SELLING

—— THE ——

TRUTH

UNLEASH THE POWER OF THE
Advisory Selling Method

PAUL ROTH

SELLING THE TRUTH

Book Design by
Transcendent Publishing

Editing by Elizabeth Baker and Lisa Traver

Author Photography by Brigitte Callieu

ISBN: 979-8-9876629-0-8

The author makes no guarantees concerning the level of success you may experience by following the advice and strategies contained in this book, and you accept the risk that results will differ for each individual.

Printed in the United States of America.

Every human conversation is a selling conversation.
Selling the Truth means telling the truth.

No matter who you are or what you do, by learning the Advisory
Selling Method, you learn practices that develop your
natural ability to sell the truth.

DEDICATION

This book is dedicated to anyone struggling to find meaning in this extraordinary world. In the end, we all want a life worth living and how we go about it determines the difference we make for ourselves, our families, our workplaces, and our world. I wrote this book so anyone can master the skills needed for self-awareness and the ability to connect with others. We will explore what selling really is and isn't so that you can step into new territory and become more effective in your approach.

You will access a level of performance you may never have dared to consider. Everything you need is already within you.

Most agents naturally want to become more of an advisor for their clients but because they don't know how, their language betrays their best intentions. We must learn to transform selling from the set of cheap tricks it has become into the sacred act it was always meant to be.

WHY THIS BOOK
IS IMPORTANT

In my work with people over the past four decades, I have learned a lot about myself, about the extraordinary strength people have, and how much of that strength remains unexpressed just below the surface. Some have shown great courage in bringing out and exposing their brilliance while others keep it inside. I do not know what you have inside of you, but if it is anything like the people I have come to know, it must be equally remarkable. My intention is to give you access to what I have learned so that you can consider putting those ideas to work in your own way. The method I use to do this is based on oral tradition and I employ alliteration, repetition, and coding shaped into a modular learning architecture. This approach allows for deeper and more permanent learning.

If it is okay with you, I will address an underlying challenge we all have as human beings which is getting the full truth out on the table. We create a story about the life we have been living and no matter our accomplishments, big or small, we see them as not enough. We discount our brilliance and repeatedly vow to do better next time, yet rarely do. When we do this, we are lying to ourselves and others. The fact is, despite our accomplishments, we find that our few moments of brilliance are swimming in a sea of shame. Shame arises when we fail to tell the truth to ourselves and others about what we've accomplished in an open, complete, and timely manner.

In this book my interest is in giving you the opportunity to embrace your moments of brilliance, and build upon them, so that you create more of them as you go forward in life. I have no doubt that you will take what I am offering and use it in a way that is right for you. The questions become: What kind of future do you aspire to have? And what actions are you willing to take to accomplish that end?

Thank you for your willingness to engage in the exciting adventure of learning how to change how you sell. Changing how you sell will change everything in your life.

CONTENTS

High performance selling comes after a great many years of trial by fire to get good at the only thing that works which is Selling the Truth.

The Advisory Selling Method offers you a highly effective, well-tested method for getting there in a bigger, faster, better way.

FOREWORD

It was in the late nineties when I first met Paul. He was working with one of my real estate agents from my new office in Florida. I had recently been offered the chance to open one of the first offices on the east coast for my company. As a successful commercial real estate agent, I had little idea of what it would take to open and manage an office from the ground up, especially in this region given that I'm from Southern California.

Paul and I connected over our knowledge and respect of martial arts, me with Taekwondo and Paul with Tai Chi. These are two very different styles of martial arts, and we were two very different kinds of people. Yet there was an immediate bond that grew stronger over the twenty years we worked together. We began in the early 2000s when my office was struggling to get from 2 million per year to 3 million. Six years later, we had grown Fort Lauderdale and opened offices in Miami, which reached 37 million in sales. Unbeknownst to us, we were entering a time in which extraordinary results became possible. It is important that you know how and why that happened.

Paul was in the early stages of creating his Advisory Selling Method after a decade of working with people and major companies developing methods for unleashing high performance in sales and management. Fortunately for me, and many others, Paul focused on selling because results can be measured easily and accurately. He has spent a lifetime formulating, merging, and teaching selling practices that are going to permanently change selling as we know it.

All the methods shared in this book have been rigorously tested in real-life situations where performance matters, and Paul's dedication to bringing out our innate ability to communicate, advise, consult, and influence, without what has come to be known as the typical "hard sell" approach, changed my life.

Paul helped me build an organization within an organization based on a culture of collaboration and learning. During that time, every member of my rapidly growing team worked with Paul both privately and in groups. Our groups were called Performance Teams. There were L-Teams for new agents launching their career, E-Teams for emerging agents, P-Teams for established agents who had become full practitioners of selling, M-Teams for mentoring agents taking on the growth of others, and S-Teams for senior agents who were building their own teams.

In this straight commission business environment, agents worked together to build a culture of collaboration in which they learned that they could make a lot more money by making less money on a lot more deals. The agents at all levels created a phenomenon which grew rapidly, and in the process, we were able to take a major market share from our competitors. Subsequently, the company provided me the opportunity to oversee and grow the rest of Florida, then Texas, the mid-Atlantic, and ultimately the Northeast.

For me, it was an adventure of a lifetime, and my collaboration with Paul was mutually beneficial each step of the way. I got to build my part of a highly successful organization, while he crafted some truly unique methods for developing people in the field of selling and management.

It was commonplace for Paul's advisory communication practices to grow someone new in the business into a top producer so they could leverage themselves into a career in management. These new leaders were then able to go into underperforming offices and apply these principles to grow their agents, their company's income stream, and their careers.

The multitude of agents and managers we worked with were able to achieve high levels of success, both for the people they led and for themselves, far beyond what they could have previously dreamed of. Paul had tapped into a wellspring of natural Advisory Selling wisdom that brought out the best in everyone, even agents who earned straight commission and needed to be selfish by nature. Some could easily take the track of being a lone wolf, but in partnership with Paul, we got them to see the benefit of collaborating with one another instead. Agents came to an early conclusion that a collaborative environment was better for leading their teams.

There was a tremendous amount of intensive work on my behalf as a leader and an enormous effort made by many courageous and dedicated agents who took the risk and began to communicate in a new way based on Paul's guidance. The foundation of the methods we adopted are expertly organized in this book, and I am pleased to let you know that anyone can now readily access them. Paul generously shares his lifetime of work that has been rigorously tested so that you as a practitioner can experience increased levels of success within a shortened time period. It has been an honor and a pleasure to witness the evolution of the Advisory Selling Method, to have benefited from the practices, and to have worked with Paul as a colleague and friend.

The Advisory Selling Method is going to change everything you know to be true about selling.

–**Gene Berman**

Senior Sales Executive and Coach

By shifting from focusing solely on the transaction side of selling to including the human side of the selling equation, selling becomes easier, more effective, and enjoyable.

AUTHOR'S NOTE
Creator of the Advisory Selling Method

Although intense, the opportunity to dig deep with individual clients not only skyrocketed their growth, it perfected my ability to teach this methodology to anyone interested in revolutionizing selling, and now it's being shared with you.

As a Fortune 100 Consultant, I led many seminars and workshops for various firms. At one point, while working as a hired-gun consultant for a well-established consulting firm, I was asked to join a project with a major cosmetics company. The consulting firm's programs were highly advanced leadership methods that were well beyond the needs of the sales people I was asked to train.

The lead consultant and I were brought in to conduct a two-day program. At the end of our first day, the lead consultant came from a meeting with the company executives. She did not have good news. She told me that if we didn't adapt our approach and shift our focus to sales and management at a basic level the next day, we would be kicked out. Instead of speaking about corporate level strategies, they wanted immediate and applicable protocols for sales and management training that each participant could use and share with their teams. The protocols needed to be easily applied by the women who would be working at cosmetic counters so they could better serve their customers.

The lead consultant asked me to make something out of nothing. Accustomed to long hours, I worked through the night and developed the beginnings of the Advisory Selling Method described in this book. On day two, I led the workshop and by the end of the presentation, I had the women, who would be directly interfacing with customers, so charged up that they were committing themselves to performance levels that the executives believed to be unrealistic. Yet, these saleswomen surpassed even their own expectations! They set a goal for $30 million in sales for the quarter, which the executives thought was unattainable, and then delivered $34 million in combined sales all because they learned a beginning version of the Advisory Selling Method.

This result led to my creative breakthrough in what it means to "sell." Since then, I've developed practices and methods that ignite business ingenuity. Some of these success stories include a company that saw their sales increase fifteenfold in just six years. A sales manager at a Japanese technology firm built a predicted budget based on Advisory Selling practices, and then doubled it each year for three consecutive years. A small tax services company doubled their revenue from $250,000 to $500,000 per week in just three months. For each of these businesses, it was a shift in mindset and the application of the method taught in this book spurred each of them to revamp their entire operation.

Ultimately, after working with numerous companies, I realized that I should focus on coaching individuals rather than entire organizations. It became clear to me that there is no such thing as an organization without people and that organizations were going overboard improving their business process but ignoring the people side of the equation. Real change in any organization happens one person at a time on the front lines, not in the ivory towers of executive offices.

When I made this shift, many of these individuals were already involved in sales, management, or business operations. One of my earliest coaching clients in the field of commercial real estate has grown his gross income from $200,000 a year to as high as $11 million gross revenue per year. In the same industry, I developed a strong relationship with another client, a manager for a west coast real estate investment brokerage firm, who was opening a new office in South Florida. He had production goals that did not seem possible. By fully committing himself to the Advisory Selling Method, he and every one of his agents grew their annual gross office revenue from $2 million to $37 million within the next six years and became a number one office of a national company.

I share this with you so that you can see what's possible for you. Let's get started.

By learning the language of Advisory Selling, we no longer battle with clients because, by Selling the Truth, we get aligned with serving their best interest, and not our own.

INTRODUCTION
CHANGING HOW YOU SELL
Reinventing Selling

This book is about reinventing the principles, practices, and processes of selling. Reinventing does not mean finding a new way of selling. It means finding the true way of selling. The normal tactics, triggers, techniques, tricks, and traps of selling dominate virtually every conversation we have and keep us from achieving the results we want and deserve. We've learned to lie to sell. We don't always see it, and when we do, we tend to ignore it because it's what we've been taught. This book aims to give you a method to bring out your natural Advisory Selling skills so you can transform how you sell from the set of cheap tricks you learned for selling lies to the sacred act it was always meant to be and selling the truth. Once you change how you sell, you will change everything in your life.

If you are a newer selling agent who is struggling to make enough income to survive and put food on the table, this book is for you.

If you are an established selling agent who has achieved a level of sufficiency in your results but feel you are stagnating, this book is for you.

If you are a senior selling agent who, after years of struggle, is now riding high on abundance in your selling results and live with a constant fear that it can all fall apart, this book is for you.

You will learn that selling is not something we choose to do or not do, it is something we are always doing, and most of us fail to see it. Many people attempt to create the impression that they aren't selling, yet selling is all we do. This includes professional selling agents as well as parents, teachers, managers, consultants, and every other human on this planet. Even you.

As you change how you sell, you no longer compromise who you are and you transform into a truer version of yourself. When you choose to become a person who is intrinsically motivated to give, rather than one focused on rabidly getting, the way people respond to you shifts dramatically. When you make this shift into being true to yourself and selling the truth, the process of selling becomes more efficient, effective, empowering, and enjoyable. It also becomes easier.

Reading this book is the first step in taking an honest look at how selling began, what it's become, and what you are selling. This will give you the perspective necessary to change how you sell. The Advisory Selling Method (ASM) is about bringing out what you already have within you so that you can dump the load of counterproductive habits you have acquired. By doing so, you will become more connected with yourself and more connected to others. Get ready to shift your entire relationship to selling and watch your results soar!

PART I
WHY WE SELL &
BREAKING FROM THE PAST
THE ORIGINS & EVOLUTION OF SELLING
We are all natural born sellers who are selling all the time.

*Every moment of every human interaction involves selling
in some form. We cannot escape it.*

CHAPTER ONE
NATURAL BORN SELLERS
Everyone Is Always Selling Something

If you are a human being, you are selling all the time; there is no escaping it. This means that you can consider yourself to be a selling agent whether or not you are selling as a professional. Selling agents across the globe struggle daily with an overriding contradiction between selling and not selling. Selling is their job, yet many hold back because they worry that they will sound too "salesy." Others are too aggressive and attack with a predatory approach. There is a great deal of uncertainty, doubt, and sometimes shame about what they are doing. Either they are a wimp or a cocky predator. Many consider getting out of the sales profession but keep holding on for the next big "win" in order to pay their bills. We all have moments of despair about selling because we don't understand what selling really is or that there is a choice between selling lies and selling the truth.

The greatest misconception about selling is that there are people who sell and people who don't. There are some people who try to disguise their intent and claim, "I'm not trying to sell you" even though it is their job. But in reality we are all selling all the time. We can't help it. We are natural born sellers. As sellers, we all have clients. If you are a parent, your clients are your children. If you are a teacher, your clients are your students. If you are a manager, your clients are your team members. If you are a selling agent, your clients are your customers.

As a human being, you are a selling agent. Once we accept this

3

truth, we can all get much better at the one thing we do more than anything else: selling. We must wake up to this reality and embrace it. We must recognize our acts of selling, whether we're promoting an ideology, a religion, a philosophy, a relationship, a new idea, a product, a service, or an asset. Everyone we encounter and engage in conversation with becomes, in a sense, a client. Every one of us is selling something to ourselves or someone else all the time.

Selling is not something we choose to do; it is all we know how to do. We are incapable of stopping it. We have become our planet's dominant species because we have perfected selling more than any other species. If you shy away from this principle, I know how you feel. I still feel that twinge of hesitation when I say I am selling. But selling is all there is in life. Rather than running from it we must get good at it and learn how to sell the truth. As natural born sellers, it makes sense for us to gain a deeper understanding of what selling is and is not. Our entire world has been built by selling, and our selling methods shape our world in every way. Meaning, that if our selling method is deceptive, we are shaping our world with deception versus telling the truth to shape the world in a positive and productive way.

The selling habits designed for selling lies that are normally taught in typical sales trainings are unnatural. Our true selling skills are natural and designed for selling truth. These natural and essential selling skills are advisory in nature. They have been buried under a pile of unnatural behaviors, comprised of tactics, techniques, triggers, tricks, and traps that distort the natural selling process and make it more difficult. As a result, many people think of selling as a somewhat degraded activity relegated to a few professionals who are trained in this frequently suspect field, who develop a mastery at manipulation and are not to be trusted.

Like actors and athletes, selling agents are performers, and since we are all selling, we are all performers regardless of what we sell. When I use the word "agent" I mean "agent of change." When an agent shows up, things change. The difference we make with one another and in our world can be measured by the amount of change that is created.

You might remember a high school chemistry experiment where you learned about catalytic agents. The teacher would mix two chemicals in a beaker where they coexisted without incident until the teacher poured in the catalytic agent. This agent prodded the other two chemicals into action, and soon they became something new. However, the catalytic agent remained separate from whatever new thing was created. Similarly, as selling agents, we engage in relationships with people concerning new ideas, relationships, products, services, and assets. When we do this as an agent of change, we cause a catalytic reaction between the people we are working with and what they are buying. Selling agents are not changed by the transaction, but without them, the transaction could not take place.

Choosing Who to Be

More often than not, people observe the facts in front of them and develop an interpretation of those facts, which is a story about the facts, and not the facts themselves. Therefore all stories to some degree contain lies that form our perceived "truth". Story can be defined as a body of interpretations based on past experiences that shapes our view of the future in a way that limits our actions in the present. This is called subjective reality. Whenever we build a story about the facts of our situation, it tends to be negative and highly inaccurate. When we separate ourselves from our story and look only at the facts, we are in objective reality. But facts by themselves rarely provide the inspiration needed to generate something new.

To do that, we must step beyond the facts into what is a more creative reality based on the truth of what can be. Only in this creative reality can truth be found, and it is not based on past experiences or limited to the facts themselves. It takes courage to sell truth that will speak a new reality into existence regardless of the evidence. To do this requires that we skate on the edge of delusionary thinking in order to ever get close to the truth. Because people live and die trapped inside their interpretations of the facts, their story becomes the lie that keeps them from discovering the freedom that only the truth provides. From truth, we can change the results we achieve by changing our actions. The only way to significantly change our actions is to change who we choose to be. Who we get to be depends on what we are selling to ourselves as shown in the illustration below:

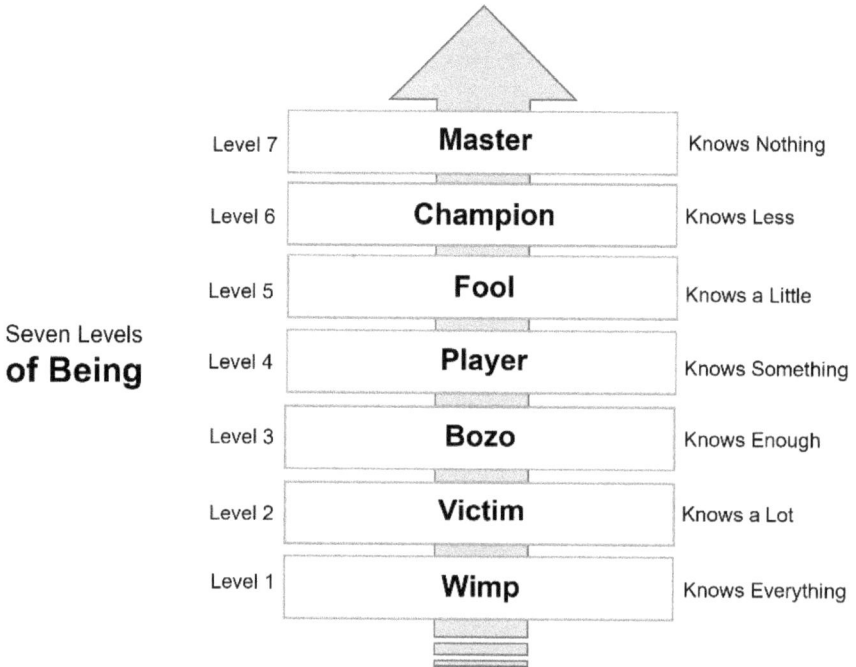

Seven Levels of Being		
Level 7	**Master**	Knows Nothing
Level 6	**Champion**	Knows Less
Level 5	**Fool**	Knows a Little
Level 4	**Player**	Knows Something
Level 3	**Bozo**	Knows Enough
Level 2	**Victim**	Knows a Lot
Level 1	**Wimp**	Knows Everything

Sometimes, a person is being a wimp, gives up easily, hesitates to complain, and knows all the answers about how things won't work. Other times, a person becomes a victim who blames others, complains about everything, and knows a lot about how tough things are. But most of us end up being the bozo who pretends to be doing what it takes, claiming to know "enough" when we, in fact, do not. Some are players who choose to, at least, do the minimum required. Others step out and risk being a fool only to become a champion or master.

One of Winston Churchill's many great moments came when he was told that the Germans had bombed Britain with six V2 rockets in a single day. His response was that it was great news because Germany now had six less than yesterday. It was in this manner that Winston Churchill spoke victory into existence as a declaration based on no evidence. In fact, there was great evidence to the contrary. What he declared was not limited by other people's stories based on their interpretation of the facts. What he proclaimed was from his own creative reality regardless of the objective reality. In essence, Winston Churchill saved the free world because he chose to be a leader who sold the truth. He therefore could sell victory to millions of people when it was virtually impossible.

Like all of history's greatest leaders, Churchill sold the truth and could turn the worst of circumstances into the best. Conversely, Hitler sold the idea that he would be victorious, but he used the evidence of his temporary military superiority to delude himself into thinking that victory was assured. He sold lies. That is why we regard Churchill to be, despite his many flaws, a great leader. Great leaders make the choice to sell a bold reality into existence, again and again.

Who we choose to be determines the reality we create for ourselves and others no matter what challenges come our way. We each have this choice in our conversation with ourselves every moment of every day. All selling conversations take place on all three levels: selling ourselves, selling others, and selling our world. Let's explore what we are up against at each of these levels and how selling works.

Selling Ourselves

The first person we sell is the one we see in the mirror each morning. This first conversation is usually about the day we have ahead of us. Will you sell yourself on a good day or a lousy one? When you do this, you probably don't recognize that you're speaking with your biggest and toughest client — yourself. We have a choice about how we speak to ourselves and that choice has the power to affect whether we recognize a circumstance as an opportunity or an obstacle.

Consider Jim, who woke up late because he had a big night out with friends and drank too much. In the bathroom he sees himself in the mirror and does not look well. He considers calling into work to take a day off, but he has already been warned about taking so much time off. He says to himself, "I have to go in but I'm not feeling well. I know my boss will see me and know what happened and give me another lecture about being more responsible. He has been promising me a promotion, but no one has gotten one for years, so it's meaningless to bother trying to impress him. I'll just have to ride it out somehow." Jim has just set himself up for a bad day, and worse yet, he will influence others to do the same.

Speaking is an act of selling whether we are speaking out loud or just in our heads. How we speak has the power to shape our day in profound ways. We speak our reality into existence by selling ourselves on a future that will inevitably occur in congruence with what we say whether it be good, bad, boring, or exciting. This reality can either be based on truth or lies. Lies are shaped by denial, deception, and delusion. The truth is creative, productive, and powerful. The life we have been given has evolved in accordance with how we have sold ourselves and others on our view of the world.

Some people can take the worst situation and turn it into their biggest opportunity. They choose to see their biggest challenges as the reason for their inevitable success. Others will make that same situation the reason for their lack of success. They look for the smallest things to justify their unhappy circumstances. They talk themselves into failure by speaking into existence only the worst outcomes. It is a way of playing it safe and avoiding looking like a fool, and it's a sure way of experiencing a lousy result.

These people sell themselves on losing a game even before it's over, and some before it's even started. Losing becomes a strange form of winning that becomes a tough habit to break. When we sell ourselves on the worst, we get the worst. When this happens, we often pull others down with us: spouses, children, bosses, and of course, clients. They all get sucked down the tube because someone they depend on, like Jim, is starting the day having a negative conversation with themselves in the mirror, selling themselves down the tube with lies. These lies are based on their interpretation of the facts rather than the measurable, observable facts themselves.

Talking Yourself
Down the Tube

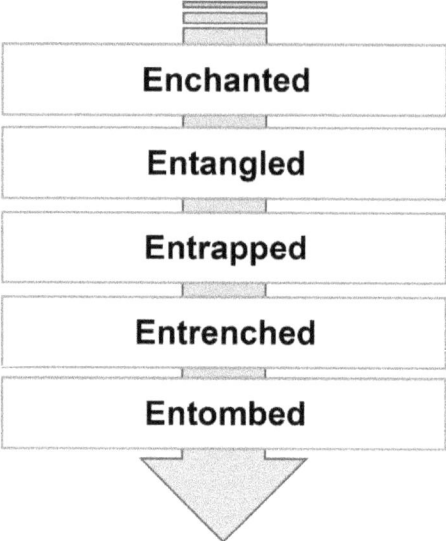

Enchanted
Entangled
Entrapped
Entrenched
Entombed

Talking Yourself Down the Tube

There are the five ways that we talk ourselves "Down the Tube." Each of these will direct our conversations to produce failure. Let's review some examples of the five steps to getting flushed down the tube using Jim from the previous example.

Step 1: Enchanted

Jim starts his first job as a new selling agent. He is enchanted with the idea of making a good income for many years to come. It all looks so easy. He is cautioned by his new manager that there will be some big challenges to overcome with clients and other agents, but Jim brushes the warning aside, ignoring the truth.

Step 2: Entangled

Once he begins calling clients, his enchantment gets shaken by tough, unfriendly, and difficult conversations. He comes to realize the clients are not as nice as he assumed they might be. Jim begins to get entangled in his thinking about how it may not be as easy as he assumed to achieve the income he had initially envisioned.

Step 3: Entrapped

Jim goes to his senior mentor to get some advice. The mentor is too busy and is dealing with challenging issues of his own so brushes him off. He is unable to give Jim any guidance or advice and Jim now builds a story about how he is caught between tough clients and a mentor who does not care enough to help. He wonders how he got himself into this situation and begins to worry that he can't leave his new job even though staying makes him feel miserable and trapped.

Step 4: Entrenched

Jim then goes to his manager who tells him that the only way to learn is by experiencing difficult conversations and tough situations. The next client that Jim interacts with is especially challenging; thus, he feels ill-equipped to build a relationship or make a sale. He talks with other new selling agents about how hard it is to generate new business, and most of them agree. When questioned by his sales manager, Jim finds himself feeling very defensive and arguing his point.

Step 5: Entombed

Jim gets back on the phone and delivers a series of ineffective pitches to clients. He becomes further entrenched in his story that he is no good at selling and that there is no way for him to succeed. He is certain he will never be any good, it is all way beyond him, and taking this job was a complete mistake. He has become entombed in the idea that there is no way this job will work out. He believes the best he can do is leave and miss the opportunity that he signed up for because it is clearly out of reach for him. Jim's story serves as a ticket for a ride down the tube. He has successfully sold himself on failure as so many people do.

The person who starts the day saying "life is good" is bound to have a better day. Because we choose the kind of world we will sell ourselves, which then influences others, it's necessary to understand the five steps to how we can alternatively talk ourselves "Up the Tube."

Up the Tube
Talking Yourself

Talking Yourself Up the Tube

There are five ways of talking ourselves up the tube. Each of these aspects will direct our conversations to produce a positive outcome. Let's review some examples of the five steps needed to rise up the tube, this time focusing on a selling agent named Eddy and his more enthusiastic outlook that leads to career advancement.

Step 1: Engaged

Eddy started on the same day as Jim, but he does not share the same interpretations about the difficulty of the job. He is fully committed to the idea that there will be a lot to learn and that it will require time and hard work. He is willing to do whatever it takes because his conversation with himself is about what can be accomplished in the future and his capability to do so, even though he has no previous experience.

Step 2: Enthused

The more Eddy engages in talking himself and others up the tube, the more he gets propelled with enthusiasm for interacting with clients. He enjoys talking with them even though some can be quite tough and not very friendly. He focuses on the good conversations and makes some notes on what he learned from the not-so-good ones. Eddy accepts that there will be friendly and unfriendly clients. He sees that the unfriendly clients are teaching him the biggest lessons, ones that will be with him for the rest of his career, and ones that he can use to produce results with more friendly clients.

Step 3: Empowered

He goes to his senior mentor to get some advice. But the mentor is too busy dealing with some challenging issues and brushes him off. Eddy recognizes that he is working with a top-selling agent with a lot of skill. He asks if he can sit in and listen to conversations with clients and he offers to take some of the workload from the senior selling agent as part of his learning process.

Step 4: Enlightened

Eddy then goes to his manager for help. He asks the manager for various ways to go about learning his new craft. When the manager gives him access to some training modules, Eddy realizes that there is a lot he can learn, and he can get everything he needs if he just asks and puts in the work. He knows that he must drive his own learning process and that he can't wait in the hope that others will do it for him.

Step 5: Evolved

Eddy combs through the learning modules and writes down a few points to test out on his calls. He gets back on the phone and delivers a conversation that includes some of these ideas. The results on the call were not great, but he sees that with practice he can get a lot better at connecting with clients, even the difficult ones. He seeks out the tough ones as the required stepping stones to his future success.

In both cases, Down the Tube and Up the Tube, at each step the selling agent makes a critical choice that determines the outcome of their internal dialogue. Since both directions are intrinsic to being human, and we can't get rid of either, it is imperative that an advisor commits to developing the skills required to move up the tube.

Talking Yourself
Down the Tube

Enchanted	Evolved
Entangled	Enlightened
Entrapped	Empowered
Entrenched	Enthused
Entombed	Engaged

Up the Tube
Talking Yourself

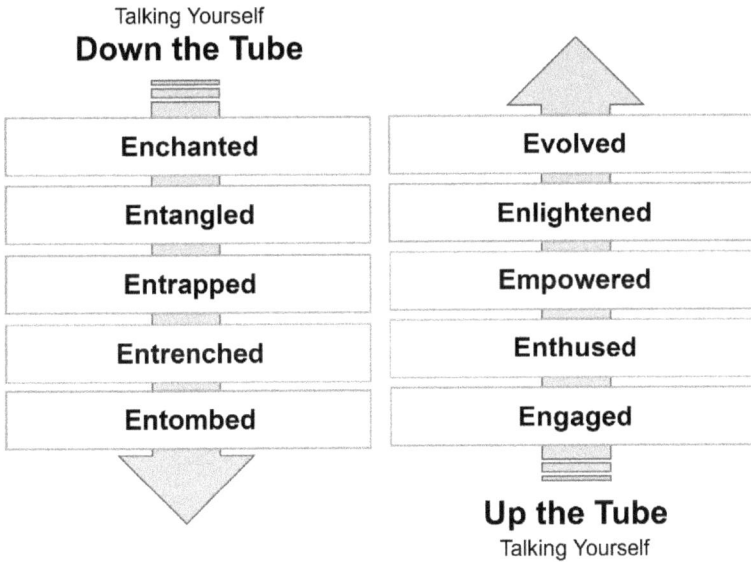

Selling Others

Once you sell yourself, inevitably you will begin to sell others, and they, in turn, do the same. Every conversation you have is a selling conversation, echoing outward to a diminishing degree, like the ripples made when a stone is thrown in a pond. In the mirror you are talking only to yourself. Yet, the nature of this conversation will have implications for others, and the challenge lies in making a choice about what kind of "mirror conversation" you will carry into your interactions throughout the day.

You can talk people up the tube or down the tube. If you sell yourself on a good day (up the tube), you will sell that to everyone you meet. But if you sell yourself on a bad day (down the tube), you will drag everyone down with you. When you talk yourself and others up the tube, you create allies. When you talk yourself and others down the tube, you create adversaries.

We go into conversations with the best of intentions, looking to create allies, but too often our language betrays us, and we create adversaries instead. The words we use, intending to draw others in, can push them away. Normal selling operates from a "get mode" that is based on some survival-driven agenda to procure and protect our own best interests. We don't realize that our words are normally geared toward competition. This competitive language can easily lead to a conspiracy to outsmart or outtalk another person. Because we want so badly to come out ahead, we may shade the truth, or even outright lie, to win.

Our lying generates conflict which corrupts our relationships with colleagues and clients. This corruption is steeped in lies and can easily become criminal. This is what is meant by survival-driven selling, which is the most common approach to selling. On occasion we find ourselves engaged in service-driven selling. This gives rise to an entirely different relationship with clients.

Normal Selling	Allies Give
Getting My Way	Giving Recognition
Getting Others To Act	Giving Others Success
Getting Paid Well	Giving Others a Choice
Getting to Look Good	Giving Others Motivation
Getting Credit	Giving Others a Chance
Adversaries Get	Advisory Selling

You access the "give mode" when you learn to access and use your natural Advisory Selling skills. This mode supports greater creativity and compassion for others which naturally leads to greater collaboration and contribution. In this way you become more consequential because you are selling the truth. Whenever people work together, rather than against each other, they always produce far more than they ever would on their own. To do that, you need to exercise compassion for the colleagues and clients you are working with. This fosters collaboration and contribution which turns an adversarial conversation into one that is more consequential to everyone involved.

Selling Your World

Every conversation has power. The idea that one person can't make a difference is untrue. Your conversations with yourself and others have the power to shape the world, for better or worse. Since everyone is always selling, you are never only an agent but a client as well. In the grand scheme of things, we each make a difference by selling. How we sell determines what kind of difference we make. Selling is so much more than "buy my product."

Selling is not a dirty word. In its simplest form, selling the truth is about giving clients the clarity they need to make appropriate choices that will lead them to the future they are looking to achieve. When we are able to harness the power of our human spirit, especially if we have a larger audience like a preacher, politician, or promoter, we create an echo that can reverberate around the world.

To be heard in the world, you must leverage the power of others by engaging them with your message so that they want to pass it on to still others, who in turn want to do the same. This is the ripple effect of the stone tossed into the pond. If you remain stuck in commonly used adversarial selling techniques, your conversations will shape a negative world around you based on lies. Because these conversations create negative or no impact, they are easily ignored or forgotten. When you develop your innate Advisory Selling skills, you will shape a world based on the truth that is bathed in contribution.

What You Can Do

The first thing to do is make a conscious choice about the conversation you have with yourself from the moment you wake up. When you look in the mirror will you choose to sell yourself lies or the truth about who will you be today? What projects will you take on and what results do you intend to produce? The second thing to do is listen to what is coming out of your mouth throughout the day and notice whether you are selling lies or selling the truth. You will begin to hear who you are being. This is an opportunity to determine if you are talking yourself up the tube or down the tube and make adjustments in your conversations. Make the choice to follow the steps up the tube. This will take a lot of practice and a new dedication to listening to what you say to others.

The third thing to do is listen to how others talk themselves down the tube and see how well you can influence them to turn their conversation around and up the tube. This will be good practice for working with yourself and your clients. Clients are often looking for how something can't work, and it will be your job to give clients a clear view of how things can work, diminishing the influence of a client's negative conversation.

By using the Advisory Selling Method (ASM), you will learn to stop selling lies and start selling the truth. You will develop your natural ability to move yourself and your clients up the tube and into an evolving relationship of partnership and collaboration.

CHAPTER TWO
WHY SELLING BEGAN
Origins & Foundations of Selling

I n ancient times, our earliest form of selling was rooted in deception. Survival required defending ourselves against formidable predators and hunting by any means possible. For instance, in prehistoric times, ingenious traps were devised to capture a meal. A prime example was the digging of deep holes in the earth, cleverly concealing sharp stakes at the bottom. A post was strategically positioned at the center. Atop this post, an enticing chunk of meat was placed as bait. A bear or another unsuspecting animal would be lured by the prospect of dinner but end up as the main course instead. The tables were turned, and the predator became the prey, all thanks to the art of deceptive selling.

Herein lies the origins of the classic form of deceptive selling called "Bait & Switch." This is a selling technique that involves conspiring to deceive as a way to outsmart clients so that we get what we want from them even if it's at the client's expense. We have been prone to selling lies ever since. This is the part of selling that many selling agents don't feel good about but are unable to avoid. It is deeply ingrained within us through hundreds of thousands of years of practice.

Let's take a more in-depth look at the origins of selling and how those origins shape our conscious and unconscious sense of what selling is and is not. Selling began when humans began. Prehistoric humans invented selling to survive in the natural world, but our world today is quite different. The natural world is not shaped by selling; it is shaped by survival. As humans we developed selling as our unique way to survive the challenges involved in the relentlessly unforgiving natural world. Selling has unarguably contributed to our success as a species and the emergence of our human world which now dominates the natural one. Selling glues the human world together, and how we sell shapes that world. Know, however, that there are two distinct types of selling that stand in opposition to each other. These are deceptive agenda-based selling, or selling lies, and commitment-based inceptive selling, selling the truth.

Deceptive agenda-based selling and commitment-based inceptive selling can be traced back to the fundamental essence of human nature and human spirit. As offspring of Mother Nature, our Human Nature is inherently survival-driven, leading to deceptive selling as a means of feeling secure in a competitive and conflicted world. Conversely, commitment-based inceptive selling arises from the service-driven Human Spirit, a noble reflection of our innate desire to uphold truths and serve others selflessly, mirroring the harmony found in the natural world.

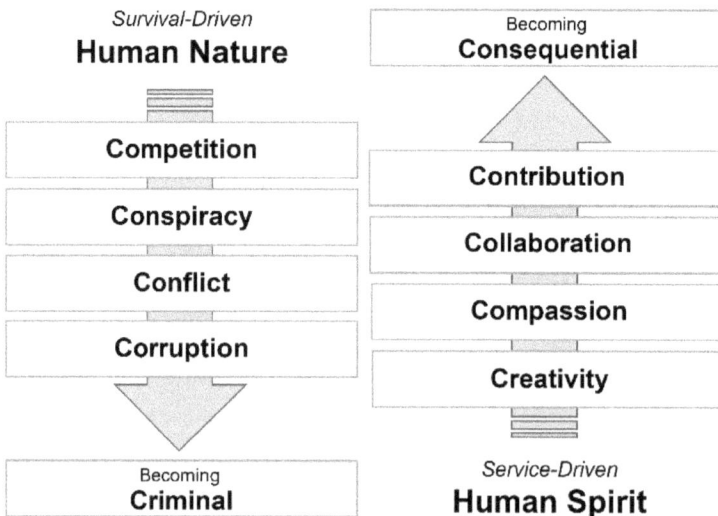

Survival-Driven **Human Nature**	Becoming **Consequential**
Competition	**Contribution**
Conspiracy	**Collaboration**
Conflict	**Compassion**
Corruption	**Creativity**
Becoming **Criminal**	Service-Driven **Human Spirit**

Since the beginning, selling has followed the laws of survival. In order to compete we used deceptive selling to avoid a physical conflict that we could not otherwise win. In addition, human beings added a layer of corruption, which is knowing that you are engaged with competition, conspiracy, and conflict, but choosing to do so at the expense of others. Continued corruption becomes criminal.

These five driving imperatives that comprise the Laws of Human Nature are automatic, mechanical, and require no conscious thought. In nature, creatures do not think about the other creatures they pursue, kill, and eat. They just do it. Survival in nature is completely mechanical. Human beings can also be mechanical when they are not conscious of their behavior. They are capable, however, of becoming aware of what they are doing and, in that moment, they are presented with a profound choice of whether or not to consciously continue the behavior. Failure to make the right choice between selling lies or selling the truth, once there is awareness, is what spawns the corruption that does not otherwise exist in nature. Unlike other creatures, human beings are aware when we are harming ourselves or others, and that it is a violation of something deep within each of us. Most creatures have little or no real sense when they are harming other species, or even their own species, they are simply mechanical in their behavior.

There is an often-told story about how a snake convinced a woman to taste a bite of an apple from the Tree of Knowledge of Good and Evil. When the woman bit the apple she did not understand the consequences. As the story goes, we are now armed with the ability to differentiate between good and evil. When we choose to ignore that voice of truth within and continue perpetrating, a fifth law of Human Nature emerges. We become criminal.

Whether casual or professional, our actions are corrupt according to some moral or legal code when we consciously perpetrate once there is awareness of the perpetration. This is the point at which criminality emerges from corruption. From there, the only outcome is becoming a criminal who seeks opportunities to do harm to others for survival or pleasure. Corruption and criminality are laws of Human Nature that do not exist in Mother Nature.

The other side of being human is called Human Spirit. This isn't the same as Holy or Divine Spirit. It is the spirit within each of us, the urge that makes us stand up and cheer when our team scores or when our child does something worthy of praise. It is where we find the courage to speak the truth. The Laws of Human Spirit are creativity, compassion, collaboration, and contribution which ultimately lead to a person becoming consequential. When a person becomes consequential, their way of being empowers others to become stronger in their ability to embrace the truth that adds value to others and their world.

It's important to note that no human being has achieved purity of human spirit. No one is without flaws due to our human nature. This is because there are two parts to being human, nature and spirit. Consider the Sphinx. Its lion-like body represents the mechanical part of our human nature. The head of the Sphinx is said to be that of a god, and it portrays our human spirit side. The two sides of being human, nature and spirit, are inseparable but often work against each other. This is happening within most people. The objective of Advisory Selling is to have them work together.

Two Sides of the Equation

The Advisory Selling Method is designed to bring balance between the survival-based transactional side of selling lies and the service-based human side of selling the truth. This means balancing the pull of human nature and the power of human spirit.

Human Nature + Human Spirit = Human Being

Let's explore these two sides and how they shape our approach to selling. Since selling is all that we do all the time, we can say that our approach to selling is our approach to life, and that shapes the world we speak into existence. Ultimately, the fate of the human world depends on what kind of world we sell to ourselves and others. Our fate is not so much in our hands as it is in our mouths. This is true whether we choose to shape a world based on lies and our survival-driven human nature or on the truth and our service-driven human spirit.

Survival-Driven Selling

Initially, human survival primarily meant protecting territory, procreating, and finding food to eat. We became masterful at hunting, fishing, and trapping. In our contemporary human world, survival now means paying the bills and looking good to others. These mechanics of survival are the primary force behind deceptive selling.

Deceptive selling is selling lies, an automatic behavior driven by our human nature. Some selling agents take great joy in, and celebrate, how they suckered a customer into buying their product even though it will cause harm to the customer. Many drug sellers, legal and illegal, are an example of this, and there are many variations of this at all levels of society. This approach to selling stems from competition. In order to win any competition, be it sports, poker, business, or politics, people easily slip into some level of conspiracy to outsmart or outdo any perceived or actual opposition. Once our conspiracies are exposed, some form of conflict erupts. It can be as simple as an argument or as complex as a world war. When we see that the conflict is harming the wellbeing of our opposition, and even ourselves in the process, we have a human choice to either continue or to refrain from causing further damage. Our failure to refrain breeds corruption and ultimately, we become criminals in the process.

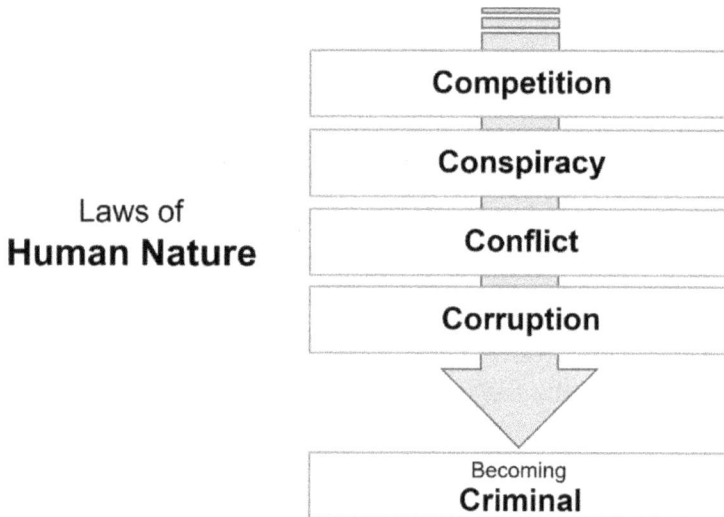

Competition

The first law of our survival-driven human nature is competition. Many companies compete against other companies to "get customers" and "win their business." Managers compete against each other to do the same. Some companies approach selling like someone might approach fishing. Deceptive selling is what happens in fishing which is based on bait and switch. We throw in a lure to attract the fish, the fish bites the bait, and gets hooked. It's no wonder why sales managers often use expressions from activities like fishing. On a crowded sales floor, an agent might jump up and yell: "I got one!" The agent is comparing his client to a fish and feeling a sense of accomplishment at "setting the hook." When the sales manager comes out of his office, he might encourage the agent to "reel them in." No client likes to be treated like a fish and feel hooked by false pretenses.

Some companies launch contests called "hunting season" and use a carnivore model for describing the role of a selling agent with an "eat what you kill" punchline. If you treat clients like prey, they will react like prey with either a fight, flight, or freeze response. They will run away, hide, change color, or attack you if they feel cornered. Clients who are treated like prey become quite skilled at outsmarting an agenda-based predatory selling agent approach.

Treating clients like fish and eating what you kill does not nurture the idea of building partnership with clients or cultivating enduring collaborative relationships. When you operate in this predatory manner, clients see how they can use you as a convenience, not as an asset. You get used, abused, and then excused. It should be no surprise that competition is a dominant feature in our world of selling. This makes selling an endless grind to find more fish, the next mark, or another sucker. If you are selling questionable products this could work very well for you. But if you are selling something of value, your product will be tarnished by a predatory approach.

Conspiracy

The second law of our survival-driven human nature is conspiracy. As in nature, there is conspiracy in business. Since the driver of business is selling, deceptive selling shapes the approach of many organizations. Companies look to outsmart their competition. They conspire to take market share by conducting intense intel on what other companies are doing.

In nature, a lynx sneaks up on a hare who has changed color to match the season. An octopus landing on the sea floor will match the color and texture of its surroundings within a microsecond. All creatures use deception in some form to survive. Animals use camouflage to disguise themselves, avoid predators, and fool prey into thinking they are safe when in fact they are not. Like all other creatures, humans conspire to outsmart others to get what they want. Deception is an essential component in any species' survival and that's why deceptive selling is ingrained in our DNA. Since deceptive selling will never leave us, we must learn to recognize it and manage it as we navigate the onslaught of selling conversations.

Conflict

Mother Nature's third principle is conflict. Trillions of creatures, big and small, eat each other every day to survive. This drive to survive puts them in conflict. When you eat chicken, you become part of this cycle. This conflict rules the world of hardcore survival-driven professional selling. There we hear talk like "win the business" and "crush the competition." It's no surprise that a big expense in many sales organizations is the legal department. The opportunity for conflict between agents, companies, and clients is huge because no matter how much they intend to work together, they are driven by laws of human nature to survive. Despite their aim, their language betrays them, and they end up working against each other instead.

Corruption

The next inevitable product of our mechanical survival-driven human nature is corruption. Almost every country, every company, every team, every family, and every person is in a battle against the pull toward corruption in our relationships and especially in selling. This is where people find that they have been outsmarted by their own human nature as they indulge in the very behaviors they preach against. There is no religious paradigm, political movement, or social program that protects constituents from this pull.

We talk about serving others, but we end up serving ourselves, often at the expense of others. We talk about protecting the interests of others when we are only protecting ourselves and allowing others to be at risk. Every one of the highest-minded global humanitarian programs ultimately succumbs to the common pull that we all feel, one that leads us toward basic corruptibility.

Becoming Criminal

It is likely that no one sets out to become a criminal, but many end up, either justly or unjustly, branded as one or incarcerated. Having spent time teaching in the federal prison system, I often saw real brilliance in people but it was misdirected down the path of denial, deception, delusion, and ultimately damage to themselves and others. Unfortunately, human beings think they are in control when the opposite is true. We are in part mechanical creatures. Even when we know that what we are doing is counterproductive, we can't stop doing it. Criminals operate with the addictive pattern of ineffectiveness which begins with the denial that something is wrong. They then deceive others that nothing wrong happened, and ultimately become deluded when they believe their own lies as the truth. This is the source of the addictive and criminal behavior that each of us is at risk of falling into however unwittingly. Everyone is lying about something. It is a fundamental aspect of Human Nature.

Service-Driven Selling

The Laws of Human Spirit are creativity, compassion, collaboration, and contribution. The Advisory Selling Method has been created to feed the human spirit which, alone, has the power to minimize corruption. People who practice the method naturally become more creative, compassionate, collaborative, and compelled to contribute. The power of human spirit turns out to be far greater than the force of human nature. Human spirit leads to service-driven selling which is based on a commitment to serving the best interest of clients and leads to having a consequential impact on them and those they touch. Everyone aspires to be consequential. Climbing that mountain is more challenging than sliding down the slippery slope of lying where compromises are required that can lead to becoming criminal.

The initial risky step toward service-driven selling is the willingness to sell the truth which requires being truly creative and going beyond the limits of common perceptions. You must then do something counterintuitive by demonstrating compassion for others. This means understanding their dilemma and being simultaneously intolerant of them achieving anything less than what they deserve.

The next level of risk is being willing to work collaboratively with others, rather than against them, and contributing to everyone's best interest, even someone you despise. When we are making a consistent contribution to others, we become consequential. This means that our thinking, speaking, and actions are based in the truth which gives facts shape, rather than being limited by our story about the facts. This truth based creativity works for the benefit of all, rather than just a few. Every human being aspires to be consequential, but most have become resigned to going along with less than they deserve to avoid the risk. It can be said that it is in this manner that human beings tend to organize their lives to avoid what they most want and deserve. Becoming consequential in the lives of others is a game changer. Those who choose this risky road reach a level of reward, recognition, and fulfillment that most never even know exists.

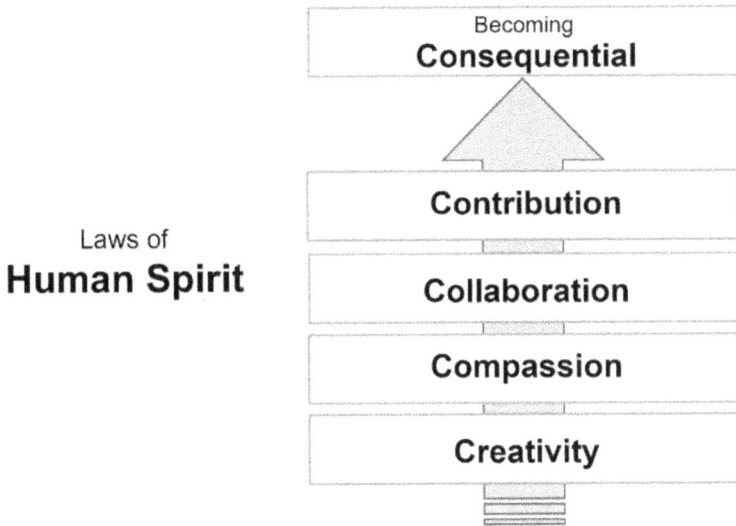

Laws of **Human Spirit**

Becoming
Consequential

Contribution

Collaboration

Compassion

Creativity

Inceptive selling is selling the truth and it expresses our human spirit. Much like in the movie "*Inception*," only a truthful message, one that will benefit the recipient, can be incepted. Inception is the opposite of deception and is the essence of selling the truth. Because it is commitment-based it is not selling for survival; it's selling to serve. We use inceptive selling to make a difference for ourselves, others, and our world. It helps us feel good about ourselves, it helps others rise above challenges, and it contributes something of value to the greater society.

Creativity

The first principle of human spirit is creativity. Creativity is an ever-blossoming flower of human spirit, until it encounters an attack from the inevitable storm of our automatic, competitive nature. It is human creativity that has built our human world and will continue to do so. The pace of that evolution is only limited by human nature. Competition, conspiracy, conflict, and corruption, squash our creativity, ideas, other people, companies, and countries.

Selling is an act of sheer creativity regardless of the side of the coin we are dancing on, deceptive or inceptive. On the deceptive side, our creativity sinks into conspiracy driven by self-interest rather than common interest. A lot of what we call creativity is just another version of conspiracy designed to outsmart others to get what we want. So much more gets created when we collaborate openly and honestly. In order to unleash our true creativity, we must first break the bonds of our endlessly competitive survival-driven thinking that mechanically turns everything into conspiracy and conflict. The Advisory Selling Method pushes these limitations aside and opens a doorway to true creativity, compassion, and collaboration to make a genuine contribution to others.

Compassion

The second principle of human spirit is compassion which is greatly misunderstood. Compassion does not mean sympathy as in "I feel sorry for you," or even empathy, as in "I feel your pain." Compassion is a unique paradox in that it combines an understanding of a person's challenging situation and an equal measure of intolerance for it being as such. Mother Teresa was a woman of compassion. She understood what it was for people to be suffering and she was totally unwilling to tolerate it. She was a woman of small stature, yet she ran a worldwide organization larger than any major corporation. She told her newly arrived nuns that she did not want them to bring their money, their knowledge, or skills. She wanted them to bring "profound joy." She was not just selling hope, she was selling the truth, which offered relief from suffering. Mother Teresa was effective at selling the truth based in human spirit but selling at this level is a rare occurrence.

In everyday selling, the best agents are advisors. In order to achieve this level of performance and recognition, you must learn how to make the shift from being an agenda-based selling agent who to some degree sells lies to being a commitment-based trusted advisor who sells the truth. They are the ones who have a real understanding of their clients' challenges and who are also unwilling to tolerate anything other than what's best for the client.

This is especially true when a client has become their own worst enemy. In this case, understanding and intolerance are required. These are the type of trusted advisors that clients return to again and again. Selling agents must learn that they cannot lose something they don't already have. Advisors take the risk to say something that someone may not want to hear, but hearing it will pave the way to a relationship built on honesty and trust. Instead of being afraid that you will offend someone, it's worth the risk to be intolerant of what isn't working for that client. If you can't risk a relationship, you will never have one.

Collaboration

The third principle of human spirit is collaboration. Some companies have shifted toward greater collaboration from within and some have even achieved greater collaboration with customers. Before we explore how this can happen, let's consider an example of what it looks like when collaboration is undermined.

One company that I worked with was a model of full collaboration in which people worked together with passion and joy. The mission of the company was one of contribution and all employees stood behind this mission. The company clearly prioritized people over their process, performance, and profits. Yet they were making billions of dollars.

Because of this, they faced the threat of hostile takeover from a larger company that wanted to buy them out. A new set of executives were brought in to protect the company from this takeover, but they ultimately destroyed the collaborative culture of the company in their effort to save it. In six short years, the monetary value of the company increased over four-fold, but the spirit of the company was lost in the process. One executive said, "We must become more competitive on the outside, and so we must first become more competitive on the inside." Rather than being taken over, they became the company that took over many others in the "kill or be killed" world of business. This once vibrant organization became a wasteland of human despair in a few short years. They made more money, but the people were miserable. This is survival-driven business, the opposite of service-driven business.

When you shift your priorities to a service-driven commitment, there is a greater sense of fulfillment in the business process. Clients, employees, and companies that work together rather than against each other turn out to be many times more productive and enduring. No one is miserable and everyone wins. Companies that choose to work together with other companies make giant strides in their industry and the world.

The ability of humans to collaborate has elevated us to become the dominant species on the planet. Working together in large numbers requires communication. Collaboration and communication are important components of Advisory Selling. One example is a regional sales manager I worked with who was employed by a giant Japanese microchip corporation. He was falling extremely short of his required yearly revenue objectives. Without any foreseeable solution and with the loss of his job imminent, he devised a creative plan that would serve everyone in the industry, himself, his clients, and other agents. Putting aside the normal competitive mindset and speaking a truth that was previously unthinkable in the world of business, he invited sales directors from major competitors to a collaborative exploration of ways to help each other succeed. These competitors were normally at each other's throats, but he invited them to take a different path, one that had never been taken before, and was based on working together. In so doing, he surpassed his seemingly impossible income budget and doubled his numbers each year for the following two years. It's no surprise that he was eventually promoted. In this example, it was the sales manager's willingness to collaborate with competitors that allowed him and his team to achieve what they achieved. To succeed at that level of accomplishment, collaborative communication is required.

Contribution

The fourth principle of human spirit is contribution. For example, the Reverend Martin Luther King sold a vision of the human spirit and fostered that vision in his followers. He planted a seed in people's minds that would benefit everyone long after he was no longer alive. Because he sold the truth that planted a seed of an incepted idea that blossoms to this day, he became an advocate for the soul of America and challenged it to rise to a level of greater creativity, collaboration, compassion, and contribution. He ultimately became consequential to more people.

Becoming Consequential

The outcome of being human-spirit driven is becoming a person of consequence whose thinking, speaking, and actions make a major difference for many people, those they meet, and still others, decades into the future. This is the ultimate condition we all aspire to reach, but we are undermined when our survival-driven human nature steps in to save the day and inevitably ruins everything good. Since we cannot separate our human nature from our human spirit, we must learn to live with both and develop our skills at balancing them, so the two work together rather than against each other.

Advisors who are focused on making the biggest possible contribution to clients are the ones who have the greatest and most lasting success. Many companies are gaining market prominence by contributing to the well-being of their customers and the world they inhabit. They choose to operate in alignment with human spirit, breaking the grip of the limitations of a world limited by human nature.

As humans, our survival instincts are deeply and permanently ingrained, which shapes our unique expression of human nature. Our human nature is only capable of deceptive selling. Deceptive selling is the automatic selling mode which is essentially selling lies. This automatic mechanical behavior cannot be reversed but it can be displaced. It is our human spirit that has the power to push aside the lies and unveil the truth. This is called Inceptive Selling where the challenge is to sell the truth regardless of the risks so your human spirit can shape your dominant mode of discourse.

Forcing Decisions Versus Empowering Choices

The two sides of selling, deceptive and inceptive, are usually at odds, challenging us to choose between survival or service, conflict or contribution, in every selling conversation. Inception, the language of human spirit, and deception, the language of human nature, are tied to each other like two sides of the same coin. The deceptive person may do some harmful things, but ultimately make some positive contributions. The person who is inceptive may do a lot of beneficial things but can also become corrupt. Both are capable of corrupt behavior and it's this that leads to the downfall of any great person, company, or country regardless of the political or economic system.

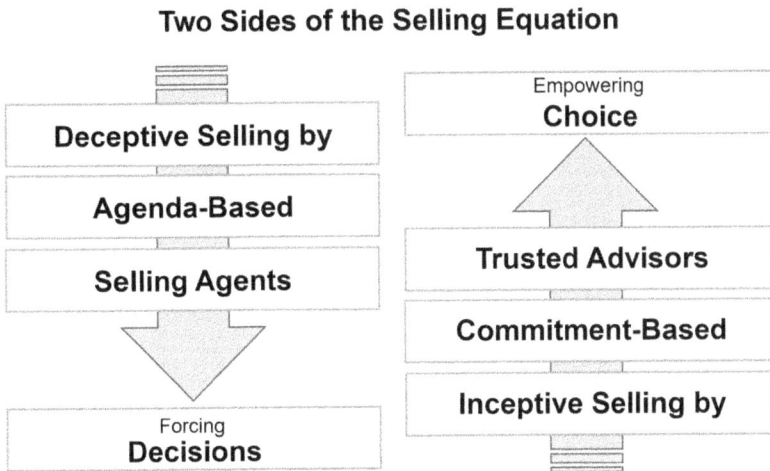

Two Sides of the Selling Equation

Deceptive Selling by	Empowering **Choice**
Agenda-Based	↑
Selling Agents	**Trusted Advisors**
↓	**Commitment-Based**
Forcing **Decisions**	**Inceptive Selling by**

Many selling agents are agenda-based and are oblivious to how often they are selling lies to get what they want. They fail to realize just how much they operate on the deceptive side of this equation in order to force clients into making decisions that may not be in the best interest of the client. Some of the more successful agents have become trusted advisors because they operate on a basis of commitment from which they sell a truth that empowers clients to make appropriate choices that serve the client's best interests. Since we can't get rid of either side, we must get these two sides to work together as we grapple with the pull of each. Unfortunately, almost all of our selling experiences and training are based on deceptive agenda-based selling even though claims are often made to the contrary. Therefore, deception becomes our dominant mode of discourse.

If we could recognize this, we would likely do something about it. But we are blind to how deceptive selling dominates the swell of conversations that make up the fabric of our human world. Deceptive selling is automatic human behavior, and it can take a dangerous turn when we pursue deception as a profession. Even if it is not something we consciously do, it can still creep into our conversations and blind us to the damage it causes.

The Advisory Selling Method is designed to bring out your inceptive selling skills, develop them, and help you apply them so you can balance the scale between human nature and human spirit and make the shift from deception to inception.

What You Can Do

To apply these principles, you must begin to listen to yourself and notice when you are employing deceptive selling and when you are tapping into inceptive selling. Notice when you're in denial about some facts and that you have a hidden agenda. That is deceptive selling. When you seek to serve your best interest over the best interest of the client, you are engaged in agenda-based selling. This pushes you into denial because people are wired to cover up their mistakes. Your denial then causes you to deceive others about the facts of your hidden agenda. You become deluded once you begin to believe the lies you tell others. If something feels wrong, it typically is. This agenda-based selling stems from our automatic survival-driven programming. This addictive pattern of basic human nature is very difficult to escape. As you develop your natural skills using the ASM, you will see your power to incept and serve grow exponentially into commitment-based advising. From there, any need for deception will diminish greatly.

In inceptive selling, notice when you are grounding your conversation in your own integrity. There are many definitions of integrity and in this case, it means being true to oneself and serving the best interest of others. This is commitment-based selling which offers a pathway to freedom from the denial, deception, and delusion that limits our performance. Only then can you be true to others and speak with authenticity so that everything is out on the table, and nothing is left out or held back. When you do this, notice how your creativity, compassion, collaboration, and contribution make your conversation with clients consequential, and once unleashed, give you the clarity needed to avoid backsliding into agenda-based selling. This is the essence and purpose of the Advisory Selling Method.

Selling may be the key to our survival as a species,
but it is shocking how little we understand about how it works.

CHAPTER THREE
HOW SELLING EVOLVED
Agenda-Based & Commitment-Based Selling

Over the past few thousand years, particularly since the invention of the bartering system and use of currency, agenda-based selling has evolved into something we all do, often unconsciously. When hunting was no longer the only necessary means of survival, prehistoric hunters transformed themselves into farmers who took food to market in exchange for other goods. Soon, money came into existence as a new medium of exchange to simplify trade and store wealth and selling became the primary force that moved us beyond survival into sufficiency and abundance. The common goal shifted from survival to the accumulation of wealth.

Throughout the course of history, salespeople have had a dubious reputation, from the merchant who was identified as a shady camel trader, to the sneaky snake oil salesman on the prairie, to the suspect horse trader. Land used to be the biggest commodity and offered the greatest opportunity for fraud. There was a time when settlers traveled for months across the plains only to find that they had spent their life savings on land that was not farmable, grazeable, or usable in any way. They further had to contend with indigenous populations and Spanish settlers who had also laid claim to that same land. Selling was a very messy affair as the United States was being transformed and colonized. When the primary mode of transportation changed from horses to trains and then to automobiles, there emerged the now ultimate cliché of deceptive selling: the used car salesman. Through the ages, selling agents like these have used a conspiratorial mode of selling lies that has earned them a reputation that makes selling suspect to customers.

None of these are meant to be blanket statements and are not always based on fact. That said, we have judgments about who we consider to be untrustworthy and that has colored the world of selling. Many of us have experienced being positioned as suspect when trying to sell our product or idea, but it's how we develop our approach to selling that will make all the difference in reversing these assumptions.

Many selling agents claim to prioritize the best interests of their clients, and while some genuinely believe this, the actuality often differs. Agents tend to overlook the fact that their primary objective is to secure clients and close sales in order to get paid. If the agent is employed by a company, their role is to acquire clients and achieve outcomes that benefit both the agent and the company, but not necessarily the client. This approach is what we have been calling agenda-based selling, where the focus is on personal and organizational interests rather than the client's needs.

On the other hand, commitment-based selling takes a different approach, which is achieved through the practice of the Advisory Selling Method. In commitment-based selling, the agent is genuinely dedicated to understanding and serving the client's best interests. This involves actively listening to the client's needs and recommending solutions that align with the client's project. For example, instead of pushing for a sale that may not be the ideal fit, a commitment-based advisor may suggest alternative options or even advise against a purchase altogether if it is not in the client's best interest.

Agenda-Based Conversations		Empowering Choices
		⬆
Posturing		Recommending
Pretending		Presencing
Pitching		Presenting
Proving		Positioning
⬇		
Forcing Decisions		Commitment-Based Conversations

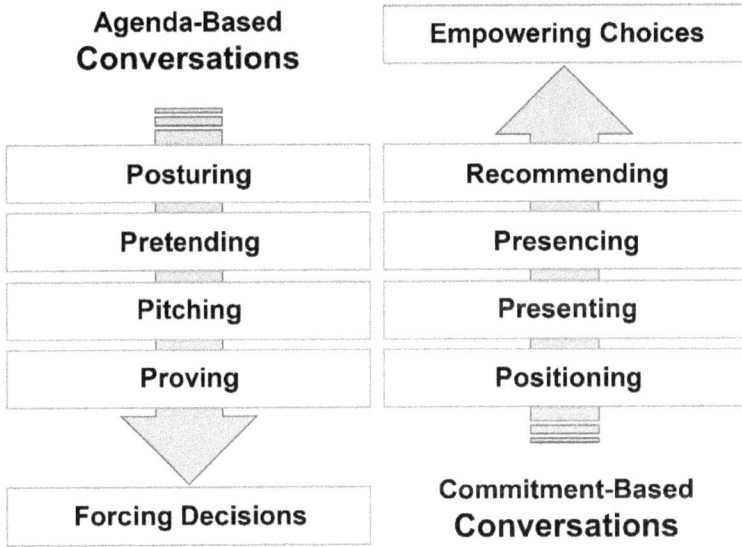

By adopting commitment-based selling, agents prioritize building long-term relationships with clients based on trust and mutual benefit. They strive to provide consistent service, offer transparent and honest guidance, and act as a trusted advisor throughout the buying process. This approach fosters client satisfaction, repeat business, and positive referrals, ultimately benefiting both the client and the agent in the long run.

Agenda-Based Selling Conversations

Most selling agents are agenda-based and out to get something for themselves. Most of the time, agents are not aware that they have an agenda because it is tightly woven into the fabric of their reality. We rarely recognize much of the agenda-based selling conversation coming out of our mouths, so our true agenda remains hidden even to us despite all our posturing, pretending, pitching, and attempts to prove the contrary. Until we identify our hidden agenda, we have little power to change how we sell and we have no power to truly serve clients. When our agenda does become obvious, no matter how much we try to shut it down, we typically fall right back into our normal agenda-based modes of selling lies that fail to fully connect with a client and their best interest. The key is to identify your agenda, detach from it, and then commit to a client's best interest. To do so, you need to better understand the five facets of agenda-based selling.

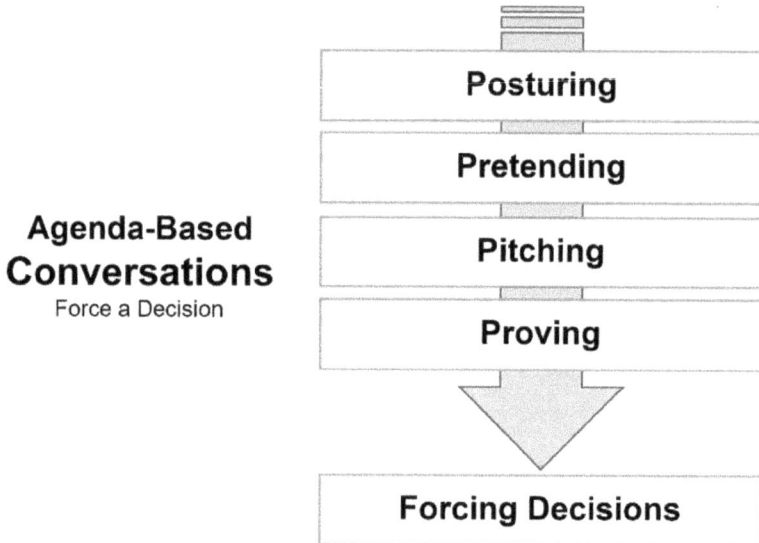

Agenda-Based Conversations
Force a Decision

| Posturing |
| Pretending |
| Pitching |
| Proving |

| Forcing Decisions |

Posturing

Selling agents who engage in professional selling start by posturing as interested in the client, when in fact they are primarily interested in their own agenda. For example, a scam artist may present themselves as a friend. Scam artists and thieves refer to their victims as "good marks." By mark they mean a person who they can easily take advantage of, someone who is easily fooled by the scammer's posturing and whose pain will be the scammer's gain.

Even in the most client-centered selling relationships, an agenda is always there, ready to seize the opportunity to get a result for the agent, and if required, at the expense of the client. Many selling agents are highly trained in the art of posturing and use the guise of friendship to get clients to do what the selling agents want. When posturing is the priority, it calls forward a lot of pretending.

Pretending

Pretending is a skill some selling agents develop so intensely it becomes a habit that is very hard to break. We are all pretending, in some ways, in some areas of our lives. This comes from a basic belief residing within everyone that they are somehow not good enough. No matter how much we have previously accomplished, we go through life living in denial and delusion. In fact we pretend so much that even we forget that it is pretense and believe it is the truth. We've been sold that "fake it until we make it" is the answer but that too is a lie.

When agents pretend, there is no chance of making an authentic connection with clients. What agents get in return is equally inauthentic. Therefore, partnership is not possible, and agents risk being positioned as a convenience. When they're no longer "usable," they are quickly pushed aside. When selling agents get pushed aside often enough, they develop self-doubt and need to pretend they have it all together when they don't. If the product they are offering does not deliver on its promises, they must also do a lot of pretending about the value of that product, sinking further into deceptive selling.

Pitching

When the foundation of partnership cannot be established, we feel the need to turn up the pressure with the intention of convincing clients to take the actions we want. Once the prospective customer, or mark, has been identified, it is time for a high-pressure pitch. A pitch is normally designed to convince clients to take action that is aligned with the agent's agenda. Most of these selling conversations begin with a detailed overview of an agent's track record, market knowledge, and team capabilities. Agents tend to pitch what they can do for the client, how they can do it better than others in their industry, and then they pressure clients into making a decision that serves the interest of the agent. At this point, clients could not be less interested, and because they feel pressured, they pretend to listen to the pitch while planning their getaway.

In addition, when pressure is applied by an agent, clients take a more adversarial posture. In this case, clients may use the pitch to gather information that they can then use on their own, or with some other agent with whom they have a preestablished relationship. Regardless, pressure pushes clients away. It never matters how hard a selling agent works on the preparation of a pitch, how beautifully they package any client materials, or how much pressure they exert when giving their pitch if the client's objectives are not prioritized.

Agenda-based, high-pressure pitches rarely connect with clients and what they need. Conversely, commitment-based presentations focus on what clients can accomplish and always make a connection. In Advisory Selling, you learn how to present to clients the options available to them and how you can help them accomplish what they want. Pressure should not come from the agent, it should come from the reality the client is facing as shown to them by the agent, as an advisor.

Proving

Agenda-based selling agents feel the need to convince clients to make decisions that the agent wants them to make for the good of the agent. This will require the agent to build a case to "prove" their pitch. Just as in a court case, proving can be a lot of work, and convincing a client like convincing a judge, isn't always easy. This level of convincing requires a great deal of deception, especially when the evidence is contrary to the claimed client benefit. The agent will need to manipulate the facts of their presentation to win the case. Deceptive selling can only go so far. Usually, it ends up as a one-time sale or with the deal blowing up. The agent is then left with no deal, no future relationship, and no referrals.

Selling agents who sell lies using agenda-based selling techniques work harder and harder for fewer results. It turns out that clients instinctively know when a selling agent is working hard to prove something and convince them to take an action that doesn't make sense. Clients get suspicious of being lied to by the agent. If the product being offered seems too good, they ask themselves why the agent is going overboard to prove the value of their offer and whether the agent can be trusted. Since clients typically recognize when promises exceed an obvious lack of value, they pull back from a transaction.

Forcing Decisions

Clients have an uncanny way of peeling apart a façade and exposing the lies which make agenda-based selling difficult, detrimental, and draining. This is because agenda-based selling agents are using their arsenal of tricks to force the client into making a decision. The Latin root for the word decision is *de-cide-re,* which means to kill off or carve out. "Cide" means to kill as in homicide, pesticide, and decide where options get killed off. It's no wonder that when an agent forces clients to make a decision, clients tend to hesitate and do nothing for as long as they can. They want to keep their options open. This is not about empowering the client. It is about manipulating, or sometimes grinding, the client into submission. Once this process has started, the agent will have to continue grinding until a deal is done. This requires unnecessary work and usually blows up in the agent's face.

The prime result of any agenda-based influence is that it usually pretends to serve the client's best interest but fails to do so, and in turn, undermines the relationship between the selling agent and the client, sometimes irreparably. This is why many agents slog through endless lists of prospects to find a few possible opportunities in ever-diminishing numbers. It can be a long, slow road to repeated failure to achieve objectives, and in many cases will lead to an inevitable career change.

Commitment-Based Advisory Conversations

Commitment-based selling is the opposite of agenda-based selling. In agenda-based selling, the selling agent is seeking to serve their own best interest by lying to a client. In commitment-based selling, the trusted advisor is looking to serve the best interest of the client by unveiling the truth.

When agents shift to commitment-based selling, clients quickly become far more receptive, engaged in transactions, and are more likely to become enduring partners. This is because commitment-based advisors are empowering clients to make a choice not forcing them to make a decision. Giving a client a clear set of options empowers the client to be responsible for making an appropriate choice that will serve their best interest, not the best interest of the advisor.

When an advisor offers three or more options, there is no longer anywhere for the client to hide as the full set of available options, the consequences of each choice, and the accompanying risk factors are laid out by the advisor selling the truth. With the truth staring the client in the face, they have no escape. The first option is always to do nothing. Putting this on the table frees the client to consider the other options. It is no longer about forcing a decision but rather about recommending the appropriate course of action that will give the client the best possible chance of getting to the future they want. If the client does not follow the trusted advisor's recommendation, that is their choice. They won't come back to the advisor and say, "You should have told me." Instead they will say, "I should have listened." A surge of new clients will be knocking on the advisor's door because the commitment-based agent, as an advisor, is offering what most clients want: a partner they can trust who speaks the truth.

Learning how to influence a client is the key to successful selling. However, this influence is typically misunderstood. You need something worthwhile to offer that does not require any tactics, tricks, or traps. Clients are not buying your product or service just because it's "good." They are buying it to get them to where they want to be, to fulfill their project. That said, once they do buy, it had better deliver on promised results. It's about ensuring that once you influence a client to make a commitment, whatever you are offering is of high quality and real value to them. To do this, there are five components to selling that must be understood.

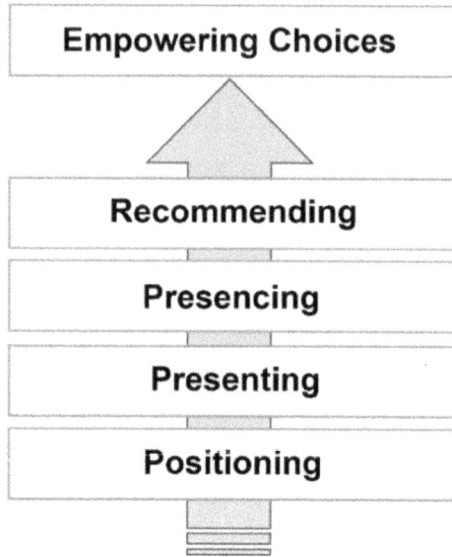

Commitment-Based Conversations
Empower a Choice

(diagram labels, bottom to top: Positioning, Presenting, Presencing, Recommending, Empowering Choices)

Positioning

It's imperative that you have a valuable offering that serves the best interest of the client so you can position it in a way that creates their future possibility and the pathway to get there. Your offer must be capable of delivering promised results aimed at moving a client from where they are now to where they want to be in the future. If you are committed to your process and fully committed to your client's project, your positioning will generate the necessary client commitment.

Presenting

There are three essential things you must be knowledgeable about to influence the actions of clients and get them to commit to forging a partnership with you in order to accomplish their project. These must be effectively presented and include knowledge of what you are offering, knowledge about the delivery methods, and knowledge about the person and what they want to accomplish once the process has been completed.

Such a knowledge base is built by gathering data, organizing it into useful information, then applying both your experience and the expertise of others. In this way, information becomes knowledge. But knowledge itself does not have the power to influence client actions regardless of how committed you may be. Building on this knowledge base, you must gain clarity regarding the client's project, the problems that could hinder their ability to accomplish that project, and the actions you are going to take to assist the client. This must be presented in a powerful manner that compels the client to make the most appropriate choices in alignment with their best interest.

Presencing

The key element in this commitment-based process is working with clients so that they get present to the truth about their project and how it can be achieved. In this context, project means projection into the future. Every client has a project, but they are not always clear about it. They may have a vague notion about what the project is, but they lack a distinct vision of the future, which is needed to take effective action. Getting from here to there is the prime objective of a project. It sounds easy in the description but is far more difficult in execution.

Recommending

Once the client has been brought present to their project, the process of getting their commitment can be established. Because the essential knowledge has been compiled and conveyed, you can take on the project with the client and deal with the problems as they emerge. You can recommend the best course of action to the client so that they can seize opportunities, deal with any obstacles, and turn them into stepping stones to their success. The problems that matter to a client are ones that could keep them from successfully making the transition from where they are to where they want to be. The trusted advisor must tell the truth to sell the truth if they hope to empower the client to solve any problems that could compromise their project. Clients are influenced by an advisor only when they see that the advisor's recommendations make it possible for them to achieve the future they want.

Empowering Choices

The most important thing about influence is that you can move clients to choose a course of action. Regardless of their doubt about the advisor's process, the number one reason clients do not take action is because they doubt themselves. In order to truly influence the pathway to an appropriate choice, the advisor must reduce the client's doubt about their own capabilities and about the process the advisor is offering. The most important part of this process is to empower clients to "doubt their doubts" and lead them to make the most appropriate choice that will serve the client's best interest to the fullest.

Selling Strategies

Selling may be our greatest gift, but it also presents us with our greatest challenges, requiring us to find unique ways to deal with them. There are four common, agenda-based strategies which unfortunately lead us towards deceit. Our selling approach is often reactive, geared towards survival. Interestingly, we tend to believe that we consciously select one of these strategies, but in reality, we default to whichever strategy selects us. However, there exists an uncommon, commitment-based strategy anchored in truth, which is foundational to Advisory Selling.

The Advisory
Selling Strategy

Authentic

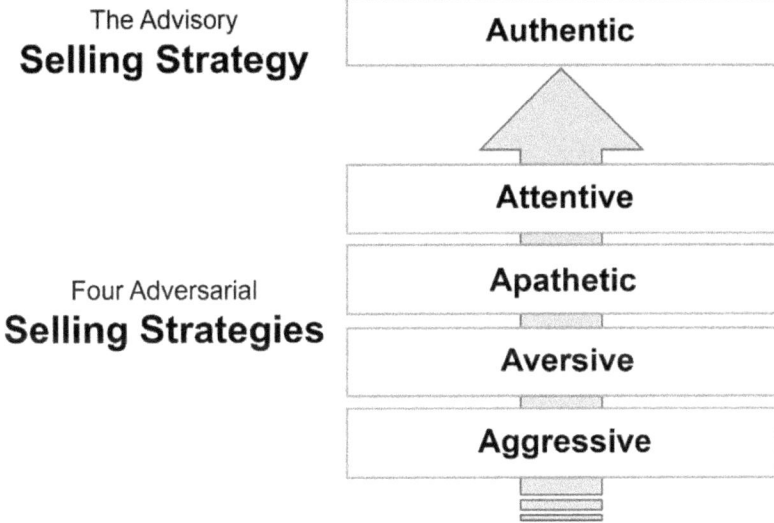

Four Adversarial
Selling Strategies

Attentive

Apathetic

Aversive

Aggressive

Four Adversarial Selling Strategies

Aggressive Selling Strategy

The first strategy, and easiest to hide behind, is the Aggressive Selling Strategy. This strategy of selling undermines long-term partnerships with clients, or with anyone for that matter. People who sell aggressively are usually afraid of the risks of a selling conversation and they hide their fear with bravado. They deflect the inevitable confrontations with clients by starting their discussions with a pushy approach that unwittingly covers up their hidden agenda which is based on lies.

Some selling agents are able to perfect the art of pushing clients to do what they want. Those who choose this approach are very interested in what's in it for them, and less interested in serving the client. These agents churn through many prospects to find the few wimpy people willing to tolerate their behavior. They soon run out of people to dominate; thus, results are very hard to come by. This is no way to build rewarding long-term relationships with anyone, nor build a successful and rewarding career.

Let's analyze this strategy with an example involving a commercial real estate agent named Tim. Tim had developed a highly aggressive, competitive approach to client conversations. While on the phone with a client who called with objections to taking an action, Tim turned everything the client said back toward the outcome he wanted and did not show an ounce of concern about the client's needs. He was known by other agents and clients as a merciless "grinder" who could overcome each and every client objection. He never let up until clients agreed to do what he told them to do. The problem with this approach was that Tim needed to work long hours to search for people willing to submit to his adversarial approach and tolerate his lies. He destroyed most of the client relationships he established, and he regularly ran out of people willing to be bullied into taking actions that would only benefit him. They would disappear, and whatever short-lived results he had previously enjoyed would evaporate. This approach only got him so far and he eventually stopped working in that field.

Aversive Selling Strategy

The second strategy is called the Aversive Selling Strategy. An example of this would be a selling agent who begins a conversation by telling the client: "I am not trying to sell you on this." This type of seller pretends that they are not selling at all when, in fact, they are. There's no way to escape selling, therefore the agent is lying. An agent who chooses this strategy is unlikely to say anything that will displease the client, even if it's exactly what the client needs to hear. If an agent cannot risk a relationship with a client, that agent won't ever keep one.

The Aversive Strategy, unlike the Aggressive Strategy, is more about manipulation than domination. Manipulation requires a degree of lying that can be far more damaging to the agent-client relationship than pushing people around. The selling agent positions themselves as a friend and ally of the client, all while leading them down the path to what the selling agent wants, even if it's of little benefit to the client. These friendships never last and the true intentions of the agent are always revealed. Selling agents using an aversive selling strategy get a reputation of being cagy schemers, never to be trusted. Word gets around the industry, and results get harder to produce as this untrustworthy reputation takes hold.

Imagine that a customer arrives for his appointment with an insurance agent he has been referred to by a friend. As they sit down, the agent asks the customer what his goals are. The customer responds that he would like a life insurance policy that would establish a legacy for his wife and children, but that he was uncertain about what type of policy would be best for him. The agent adamantly expresses that he is in no way trying to sell a particular policy, but he did want to talk about a new choice that was popular with other clients. The agent then pulls out the paperwork for three options for the customer to consider. There is an affordable option, a mid-range option, and one that is a bit pricy. The customer says he likes the price tag on the least costly option but is not sure if the benefit to his family would be sufficient. The agent repeats that he is not trying to sell one policy in particular, yet he proceeds to argue why the customer should consider the mid-sized option as it balances price and benefits. He then goes on to say, "If I were to recommend an option that would give the most benefits based on what you are seeking, I would recommend the most expensive one." The agent lies again when he further states that although he isn't looking to sell this customer a specific policy, it sure would be a shame not to get the best coverage possible and that no expense is too great when it comes to taking care of your family. That is, of course, the purpose of insurance, right? The customer who now feels manipulated by this guilt trip is frustrated that his true needs are not being served. The customer proceeds to purchase the expensive option and, many years later, reflects on how difficult it has been to make the payments despite the promised benefits. This customer never refers this agent to anyone.

Apathetic Selling Strategy

Among those using the third strategy, called the Apathetic Selling Strategy, are some luxury car dealerships, exclusive jewelry stores, and high fashion outlets. Their selling agents tend to act aloof and superior to their customers. Over time, these agents develop a habit of looking down on customers. In addition to acting indifferent, these agents take an apathetic approach that makes customers feel as though the agent believes they lack the ability to afford the purchase; hence, inciting the client to prove they can afford it, and so they buy. This patronizing attitude is their vain attempt to intimidate clients into making a purchase while at the same time avoiding the confrontation that selling inevitably brings.

This can chase many potentially good clients away, leaving these agents wading through a sea of what they consider to be unworthy customers to find the few that meet their standards. An apathetic salesperson wants you to think that he or she doesn't care whether a customer makes a purchase or not. This pretense is just another form of lying. This is their strategy for making whatever it is that they are selling more appealing. The opposite result is usually produced.

Let's consider a customer who walks into a high-end car dealership to potentially buy a car that most people cannot afford. The selling agent he approaches seems a bit standoffish, but he assumes that is all part of the exclusive nature of this brand. As they talk, the agent seems to question the customer's ability to afford such a car given the hefty price tag and questions his ability to maintain the vehicle as required. When the customer asks if the agent is trying to talk him out of buying the car, the agent simply says it was no concern of his and that it is the customer's prerogative. When another customer enters who the agent recognizes as a major buyer he has worked with in the past, he excuses himself from the initial customer and goes to talk to the person he believes he could sell to. That conversation continues and it becomes clear that the agent is not going to return, at least not any time soon. The first customer leaves feeling dejected and slighted. He determines that this is not the car for him, and he will never speak highly of that brand again.

Attentive Selling Strategy

In the fourth strategy, called the Attentive Selling Strategy, selling agents subvert themselves to continually please their clients, regardless of how outrageous those clients' demands might be. Selling agents employing this strategy are choosing to be used, abused, and excused at the client's whim. In every instance, this agent rushes back to appease the client, to do whatever is asked, regardless of the demand. This agent might run personal errands for clients or perform other favors that have nothing to do with the sale. Selling agents choosing the attentive strategy are going overboard to avoid upsetting a client. They believe their actions will strengthen their relationship with the client when, in fact, the opposite is true. By devaluing themselves, they devalue their services. Few overly attentive selling agents ever reach high-performance levels. When their performance wanes, they try to correct it by doing even more to please, taking them further down the tube. In the end, they get nowhere. Clients start thinking of these agents as mere conveniences who offer little value. These selling agents are easily dismissed because they are not viewed as an asset who commands respect and attention.

Let's imagine a newer agent who begins working with a much larger client than he is accustomed to working with. This feels exciting to the agent who is hoping that his career is about to level up to a new income bracket and an entirely new class of clients. This new client is very demanding and requires the agent to do a great deal of work above and beyond the call of duty. The agent does so just to please the client and avoid losing the opportunity. The more he pleases the client, the more the client asks him to do. This cycle goes on for quite a while and, when it comes time for a transaction, the client asks the agent to reduce his fee which the agent agrees to. It isn't until the agent is picking up some packages for the client that he realizes he is being used. When the agent brings the packages to the client, he says he can no longer do these favors for him anymore. The client tells him that he has another agent in mind anyway, that the deal is off, and asks the agent to leave.

However extreme this may seem, this is a mistake selling agents can make in their quest to please clients and grow their business. To exemplify this point, imagine a public restroom. When you need to use this facility, you choose an open stall or urinal. The point is this: you choose what's convenient, flush, and leave. Selling agents who position themselves as overly convenient get used and flushed in the same way. Overpleasing clients will never garner respect, and it is no way to assert the leadership clients need from a trusted advisor in order to make good choices.

The Advisory Selling Strategy

Authentic Selling Strategy

The final strategy, which is the ultimate selling strategy, is the Authentic Selling strategy. This is Advisory Selling at its best. Being authentic means that you are selling the truth. The question is, how authentic can you be when you're selling?

Agents who develop an authentic selling strategy can be straight with clients, telling them everything they need to know without being pushy, subversive, aloof, or a doormat. This includes telling clients the truth that they may not *want* to hear but *need* to hear. Being authentic isn't always easy, but it is necessary. Agents become a trusted advisor when they choose to execute an authentic strategy. To do so, they must become adept at risking their relationships with clients in order to build those relationships. This honesty helps them build strong partnerships that last for years, even decades. Clients want their advisors to be forthright, even when they are afraid of being challenged. They want to hear the truth. The Authentic Strategy can cut through the client's BS (Big Story), stop the delusion, and get to the truth of a situation. When this happens, the client is empowered to take appropriate action that will serve their best interest. This is the commitment of Advisory Selling.

Let's explore an example where an advisor is making a business development call and speaks with a client who says how happy he is that the advisor has called him. This reaction is a far cry from the usual level of protective listening that advisors are used to encountering. The client says he wants to move into a transaction immediately and is eager to change his situation. Most selling agents would jump at the opportunity to close a deal right away. Instead, this advisor pauses and suggests that he should meet with the client to discover more about his situation before making any rash decisions.

In their meeting, everything about the deal makes sense and the client will profit at least $2 million from the transaction. The client is ready to go forward, but the advisor pauses again, encouraging the client to take a closer look. He then asks the question, "What are you looking to do once this transaction is complete?" The client says he wants to retire and live off the profits. The advisor presses a bit further, pointing out that the client is now 73, and asks if the client plans on being around at least another 20 years. The client says, "Absolutely!" The advisor then asks if $100,000 a year would be enough to live on. The client says, "No way!" The advisor suggests that they need to talk further.

In the previous example, the agent could have seized the ready opportunity to start the transactional process during the initial call. If he had taken the deal without such an authentic conversation, the client would have gone along, but when he found out what he was headed for, it likely would have blown up at the end. Rather than jumping at the chance to go for a check, the agent, as an advisor, chose the more authentic route of telling the truth. And, as it turned out, they closed the deal. The advisor set the client up to win and, as a result, the agent shared a long-standing relationship with the client who recommended him to many of his friends.

As an advisor, the agent was smart to take a deeper dive into the client's future because, had he not, the client would have at some point come to the realization that he would have been stuck with limited financial resources for the rest of his life. If he had chosen to move forward with the deal, he would have no doubt regretted his decision, blown up the deal, and blamed the agent. Having a deeper, more authentic advisory conversation, regardless of client enthusiasm, is an essential practice of Advisory Selling.

In an authentic Advisory Selling conversation, everything must be considered. As advisors, agents must be willing to say the things clients need to hear, even when the outcome of a conversation could backfire on the agent. Establishing trust is more important than being the nice guy.

What You Can Do

Change your strategy. Your default selling strategy is automatic, and unbeknownst to you, it has chosen how you communicate with clients, but you can choose to pick your own. You can shift from operating as an agenda-based selling agent to being an authentic, commitment-based trusted advisor.

The first four normal selling strategies are influential in their own way, but the authentic strategy is the only one that fosters collaboration with clients because it embodies Advisory Selling. It always starts with an advisor's commitment to serve the best interest of the client at all costs. You must choose the authentic strategy, which is Advisory Selling, in order to provide a way to connect a client with their vision. While this vision of future possibilities will compel a client to act, it must be the inception of a truth that is clearly achievable, otherwise it will be a deception.

Clients are best served when they are empowered to make smart choices rather than have an agent trying to force a decision on them. When you choose this approach, the client always wins. When the client wins, you win.

I invite you to consider moments when you've found yourself using any of these selling strategies. I promise that as you loosen your grip on the four common selling strategies, you will unleash your naturally authentic selling skills. Only then can you move toward a more truth-based authentic selling strategy, which is the essence of the Advisory Selling Method.

PART II
HOW WE SELL &
CURRENT SELLING CHALLENGES
Trading in Adversarial Habits for Advisory Skills

Because we sell all the time, we think we know what we are doing.
The big surprise is that what we think we're selling
is not what clients are buying.

To best serve clients, the conversations we have with ourselves need to be based in truth before attempting to influence others.

Chapter Four
What We Are Really Selling
Influencing Clients to Take Action

Selling agents are never selling what they think they are selling because they completely miss what a client is buying. All people struggle to sell their ideas, relationships, products, services, and assets, thinking all the while that what they are selling is what customers and clients *want* to buy. This chapter is designed to help you understand what your customers are really looking for. I challenge you to set aside your current beliefs, embrace new thinking, and consider a more viable option that you may have never considered before. If you do, the selling experience will become easier, more enjoyable, efficient, effective, and empowering to you and your clients. And you'll make a lot more money.

Most agents who sell think their prospective customers are buying the items being offered. Nothing could be further from the truth. It does not matter how good the product or service is, how well it is presented, or how persistent and passionate you are about it. Commitment-based trusted advisors don't determine what a client wants to achieve. Trusted advisors help their clients see, and then shape, the client's vision and influence the client to see how what the advisor is offering can help them achieve that. If you don't work with a client to elicit from them what they really want, both you and the client are handicapped from the very start.

Influencing Action

There are specific aspects required for an agent, as a trusted advisor, to influence a client. Understanding how these aspects work, and what they accomplish, is essential if you are to influence the actions of others as intended. Everyone wants the capacity to influence others, but there needs to be a better understanding of what is necessary to make that happen.

Influencing Action

Consultative Selling	Action	Advisory Selling
Solve a Problem	Influence	Accomplish a Project

Knowledge Base

Knowledge
Information
Data

If you consider that your job is to influence clients to take an appropriate action, then you must make sure they see a clear pathway as to how that future will be achieved. Otherwise, the vision of the future remains a pipe dream that will never be fulfilled. Influence cuts through all layers of doubt, fear, and mistrust. Receptivity to your influence will always be based on the client's trust in you and your team's ability to deliver results.

Think of Influencing Action like a camera on a tripod. Knowledge is the first leg of that tripod, and like the foundation of a building, knowledge is essential to providing a basis for influence. Some say knowledge is power. If that were true, the world would look quite different. It is only a platform to be built upon.

To build a knowledge base, you must gather data, organize it into understandable chunks of information, and then apply your experience and expertise. This knowledge base, which can now support influence and action, is essential for an agent, as a trusted advisor, to have the power to influence clients, especially if they are hesitant to act.

The second leg of the influencing action tripod is the ability to solve complex problems. When problems surface, you must assume the role of a consultant tasked with finding solutions. Your ability to provide solutions is essential to building client trust, giving them more confidence in the success of your process. If you do not know your transactional process, it is likely that clients will know more than you do about how to solve their problems. Selling agents who place themselves in such a position of weakness leave themselves open to being used, abused, and excused like many other agents who have also failed to learn the nuances of a complex transaction. This is true even for the simple sale of a product to a customer who wants and needs the product. You will not be judged solely by the content of what you say, but by the quality of your delivery, which can only come with practice, persistence, and passion for the industry you have chosen.

The third and most indispensable leg of the influence tripod is accomplishing the client's project. When we say project, it means a projection into the future to a desired destination. It is the job of an agent, as an advisor, to clarify the project and assist a client in getting from where they are now to where they want to be. Even with a solid knowledge base and strong transactional problem-solving skills, you will never be able to influence a client to take an action unless their project, and its future possibilities, are made evident. The destination is important, but it's only a fantasy unless the path is made clear. If a client does not have a project, you will not influence them in the direction of a transaction, and the deal will fall apart before your eyes.

Therefore you need to adopt the true definition of selling:

> ## Definition of Selling
> Working with clients to <u>create</u> a vision of a future possibility compelling enough to change their actions in the present.

Humans are wired to move from where they are to where they want to be, whether that be in a career, relationship, or space exploration. There's no such thing as a client who doesn't have a project. They may not see it, but it's there. It's your job to help them recognize it, not so much to get paid, but to help them get to where they want to be in life. Once you prioritize helping someone achieve something they couldn't on their own, a paycheck will always follow.

Some sales trainers talk about finding the client's pain point. That may be included in the process, but it's not what moves clients to take action. Most people will wallow in their misery forever, but the moment they see a new future possibility, the commitment to take action becomes irresistible.

The role of the agent, as an advisor, is to work with the client to draw out and, if necessary, create that vision. It is not the advisor's role to execute that vision. The advisor's proper role is to help the client define, clarify, and take the actions required to make their future possibilities a reality. The trusted advisor becomes the catalyst that causes a reaction that will change the client's world permanently, bridging them from where they are to where they want to be. This is a huge responsibility that most agents are either unaware of or take for granted. Once the client's vision is clear, they become unstoppable in the pursuit of their objectives.

Clients are not always capable of constructing a clear vision of the future. As a result, they become averse to taking action and will resist even talking about it. If they have a vision, it may be clouded by their denial, deception, and delusion about their challenges and what it will take to get to a seemingly unachievable future. Unless the agent, as an advisor, provides the leadership to help the client see the pathway clearly, any transaction, no matter how solid it may seem, is at risk.

Consider a center fielder attempting to catch a baseball. If the batter hits a homerun just over the fence, that centerfielder risks slamming himself against the wall in an effort to catch the ball because it seems possible. If, however, the batter hits the ball deep into the second tier, the catcher does not risk banging himself against the wall. This goes for clients as well. Taking action is triggered by a vision of a future possibility that is achievable. Not having a clear future possibility leads to no action, no income, no exception.

What Clients Are Buying

When we go to a shoe store to buy a new pair of shoes, we do not walk up to the counter and ask for two pounds of leather. Obviously, shoes come in many sizes, shapes, weights, materials, and colors. We are not there to buy the stuff shoes are made of. We are not even there to buy shoes at all, regardless of who the designer may be. We are there to fulfill a specific vision and the shoes are only a means to that end. That vision may very well be to look good and feel good at work and at client meetings so that we are positioned to make more money.

Let's consider a person who walks into a shoe store. He browses through the racks, searching for shoes that he likes. Suddenly, he notices a pair of shoes that fits his vision. This prompts him to reach out and grab them, hoping they will help him make a good impression when he meets with clients. When he finds the specific shoes that connect with his vision, he'll wear those shoes until they get old. If there isn't a clear connection between this buyer's vision and the shoes, he may purchase a pair, but they will soon become part of the clutter at the back of his closet and never be worn. Look in your own closet to see how true this is. When you find a pair of shoes that truly fulfills your vision, you will gladly pull out your credit card. Why? It's not because you're buying a pair of shoes. It's because you are buying the vision of how the shoes will make you feel and how others will perceive you, and that is why you will spend the money. It's the vision that you are buying. The shoes are only a means to a future that you aspire to achieve.

In the Advisory Selling process, as advisors, agents work with clients to create a vision of a future possibility compelling enough to change their actions in the present. A client's vision may involve a major life change such as shifting from an active career to a less intense work schedule or retirement plan, or expanding and diversifying their business objectives. When someone purchases a product or service, they are driven by their vision of what it will do for them in the future, not the product or service itself. So it comes as no surprise that clients are not interested in you as the selling agent, your transactional process, or even how great your product may be unless they clearly connect with your ability to help them see their vision and fulfill those future possibilities.

What do we mean by "vision of a future possibility?" This is not some dream with an impossible outcome. It's not wishing to build the highest skyscraper or hoping to ride a spaceship to Mars. Though such dreams are technically possible, no one's resources are unlimited. In almost all cases skyscrapers and trips to Mars are fantasies rather than real visions of achievable possibilities.

For example, it is possible, with unlimited resources and time, to build an exact replica of the Empire State Building in the middle of Des Moines, Iowa. This may not be a good idea, but it is possible. It is not possible to build one that stretches between Earth and Mars, expanding and contracting throughout the year, and occasionally passing through the sun. People who claim that anything is possible fail to see the difference between what's possible and impossible. Only what is possible is possible, otherwise it is, at best, a dream. Once clients have a clear vision of the future they want that's achievable, it is essential that the trusted advisor shows them how, through working together, their vision of the future can be fulfilled.

Remember, clients are not paying for the product agents are selling. They are paying for what becomes possible for them by purchasing the product. Clients are generally most interested in themselves and how to get from where they are today to where they want to be tomorrow. As far as a client is concerned, the role of the trusted advisor is to help them get there. If they sense that the advisor is capable and interested in assisting them in this transition, then a partnership is possible. If they don't, the relationship will never develop.

Another way to think about this idea of future possibility is to consider a typical bridge crossing. Tens of thousands of people regularly cross the George Washington Bridge from New Jersey to Manhattan, and they pay over twenty dollars every time they do it. The question is, why would that many people pay that much money every day of the week to cross a very old bridge? The answer is that Manhattan is on the other side with jobs, people, dining, shows, sporting events, museums, and other exciting things to do. If there was only more of New Jersey on the other side of the bridge, they would not pay the toll.

Much like the example above, when working with clients, it is essential that you uncover their true project, what's on the other side, and that they see you and your offer as the bridge to get there. This is a challenge for selling agents who are insecure in their abilities and feel as though they must establish credibility and prove their worth to connect with a client.

Ironically, clients are rarely interested or impressed by individual agents, a company platform, or a brand unless it connects with the client's vision. You become interesting to your clients when you shift your focus away from your agenda and onto their project. It's only when clients see that you are truly interested in them, and not trying to prove how interesting you are, can you forge lasting partnerships. Selling agents who shift their attention to the client's project become trusted advisors.

Consider this: An agent created a postcard that said, "Last year I sold $60 million in real estate." Is this a demonstration of interest in potential clients? No. It's simply an attempt to be interesting to a client. The postcard could have read "Last year I helped my clients sell $60 million worth of real estate in this market." Subtle change, major difference.

Once you better understand that this is the true nature of selling, and you learn the language that positions you as a true advisor and not just an advisor in name only, you face an even bigger challenge: being heard. As trusted advisors, selling agents must deal with the reality their clients are facing. The crushing onslaught of day-to-day business can keep clients from connecting with agents. Agents must reposition themselves as commitment-based advisors so that it becomes clear to the client what the client really wants. The Advisory Selling Method is designed to cut through a client's distractions and denial about their situation to get to the truth about their vision. Only then are you able to establish a foundation for partnership that will accomplish their project.

Modes of Influence

As selling agents develop their normal selling skills, they are constantly on their toes to apply the right mode of influence so that clients take action. This is usually one that is survival-driven. When one mode does not work, typical selling agents quickly shift to another mode until they find one that does. There are four common adversarial agenda-based modes of influence that selling agents are prone to bounce between. This is normal selling which always involves some degree of lying to influence a client's actions to serve the best interest of the agent. When we step beyond normal selling, we find a more natural service-driven form of selling. This is commitment-based selling.

Learning how to influence a client is the key to successful selling. However, this influence is typically misunderstood. It's really about ensuring that once you influence a client to make a commitment, that whatever you are offering is of high quality and of real value to them. You need something worthwhile to offer that does not require any tactics, tricks, or traps. Clients are not buying your product or service just because it's "good" but also because it moves them toward fulfilling their vision. That said, once they do buy, it had better deliver the promised results. To do this, there are five modes of influence that must be understood.

The Advisory
Mode of Influence

| Eductive |

Four Adversarial
Modes of Influence

| **Seductive** |
| **Reductive** |
| **Deductive** |
| **Inductive** |

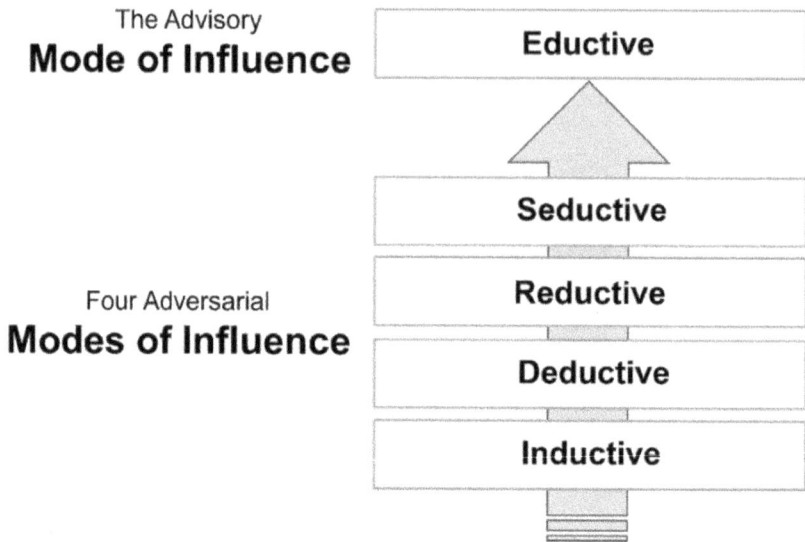

Many selling agents have automatic defenses against the confrontation that is basic to every selling conversation. To minimize the risks, selling agents turn to the four common adversarial agenda-based ways of dealing with perceived or real selling challenges that accompany any effort to influence client action. We all have one of these as our dominant mode of influence. There is also one uncommon commitment-based mode of influence that trusted advisors can choose when communicating with others. The strength of the agent-client relationship is determined by how conversations are conducted.

For example, when a selling agent who first tries an inductive approach to scare a client finds that they are not sufficiently influencing the client, the agent may shift to a deductive approach and explain everything in grueling detail, hoping that the excessive description will influence the client to take action. If that doesn't work, they may drift into a reductive mode in which they make the client feel stupid or small in order to embarrass them into taking action. Failing all of these, they might finally resort to a more seductive mode, which involves bribing a client into taking action by giving up part of the agent's fee or making extraordinary accommodations.

The only way off this agenda-based hamster wheel is to shift into an eductive mode of influence in which the trusted advisor brings out the commitment of the client to take an action that is in the client's best interest and not their own. Let's explore each of these modes in more detail.

Four Adversarial Modes of Influence

Inductive Influence

This mode blasts through a significant number of clients, only to leave behind a trail of dead deals and relatively few results. The Inductive Mode uses the threat of a negative outcome or undesirable future to get clients to act the way selling agents want them to.

Remember, we are all selling agents. A parent may threaten a child with a time out, a teacher may threaten to expel a student, a manager may threaten to fire an employee, a consultant may threaten to halt work, or a professional selling agent may threaten a client with a negative forecast of the future. All are trying to induce their respective "client" to conform with what the "agent" wants, whether it is in the best interest of that client or not.

When such a selling agent gets a call from a client who objects to a course of action or who wants to back out of a deal, they typically respond by controlling the conversation to overcome the client's objections. No matter what the client says, whether to gain sympathy or advocate for their own best interest, the agent dominates the selling conversation by threatening future consequences meant to scare the client into acquiescing. Regardless of how long it takes, the agent will grind the client down until they comply with the course of action promoted by the agent. When the inductive approach is not sufficiently influencing a client, a selling agent might shift to a deductive approach.

Deductive Influence

The Deductive Mode involves overexplaining to get people to act as we want them to. Droning on with excessive detail can become tedious for clients, but it is designed to wear them down so that they become worn out, exhausted, and finally give in to what the selling agent wants them to do. These long explanations may also feature some bits of misinformation and deception.

Parents, teachers, managers, consultants, and agents have all been guilty of overexplaining and providing excessive reasons and, in so doing, killing an idea or a deal. This is the mode parents use to nag children to take out the trash, only to have to repeat it day after day, until the parents start taking it out themselves. A teacher using this mode overexplains an assignment, confusing their students so much that they lose interest. A manager will impose systematic retraining for an employee who does not really need it. This wastes time that could have been spent more productively, leaving the employee deflated, invalidated, and frustrated. A consultant will wear clients down with lengthy selling conversations and an overabundance of paperwork. This puts the deal at greater risk each time they add more to the pile.

A selling agent may overexplain a process to the point that it no longer has anything to do with the client's vision of the future, thereby losing the client's interest. The more the client questions why the agent is overwhelming them with details, the more the agent is required to make up a story about how important it is to do so. This mode of influence inevitably requires a lot of pretending, only to produce limited results.

Because this selling agent believes the only agenda that matters is to get a deal done and get a check, they deceive the client by using intricate explanations to achieve this end, whether the client understands or not. The biggest problem with this is, once an agent lies repeatedly, they believe their own deceptions. They become deluded and begin selling a reality that can never be achieved, losing many customers along the way. Clients who see this pull out of a deal, and those that don't, get burned and never come back.

Reductive Influence

The Reductive Mode is when a selling agent makes a client feel small, often embarrassing them, in an attempt to persuade them to act as they want them to act. When the inductive bullying mode does not work, and the deductive explaining mode fails to move a client, then the next choice is to put the client down and make them feel stupid.

It is shocking how much clients are willing to put up with from agents who pull every trick in the book to get a check for themselves at the expense of the client. It is more shocking how some selling agents make the Reductive Mode their dominant way of interacting with others. Once again, this applies to everyone—parents, teachers, managers, and consultants—not just professional selling agents.

To get a child to measure up, a parent might make derisive comparisons between the child's poor choices and the good behavior of other children. A teacher may put down a student's performance, comparing it to other, more successful classmates. A manager may compare his employees' outcomes with those of employees at other firms. A consultant may devalue a client's ideas in order to get his own ideas sold. The selling agent's strategy is to make clients feel so embarrassed that they take the action the agent needs them to take in order for the agent to get a check.

Seductive Influence

The Seductive Mode uses incentives or bribes to seduce clients to act as selling agents want them to. When all else fails, and threatening, explaining, or diminishing people does not work, agents revert to the only remaining agenda-based option, seduction. Because of this, the act of bribery ends up being the most prevalent mode of influence. All of these common modes of influence are ineffective because this is where you allow your weakness to drive your actions, sending yourself and your clients down the tube.

An example of this is when in an effort to get a child to take desired actions, a parent might offer the incentive of a new cell phone or a trip to a theme park, but this is no guarantee of results. To entice a student to write a report that meets expectations, a teacher may offer a gold star. This is a temporary form of gratification that only lasts until they don't receive accolades on the next assignment. A manager may offer a bonus to any employee who exceeds projections, but without clear conditions for future performance, the employee rides the wave of adoration and begins to slack off on the job. A consultant may offer free time, or a selling agent may offer to reduce their fee, but then these reductions become a future expectation of the client. Over time, the client will feel that the agent's value has decreased because by lowering their fee, commission, or reward to accommodate and please the client, the agent's value in the eyes of the client begins to diminish. All seductive offers inevitably become expectations for the future. If the agent is unable to fulfill the elevated or unrealistic client expectations, this will cause the relationship to end.

The Advisory Mode of Influence

Making the shift away from the common adversarial modes of influence and operating in the advisory mode requires that we understand the difference between imposing our ideas and drawing out the ideas of others. To draw out is the art of eduction.

Eductive Influence

Although this mode is less commonly known, the Eductive Mode is at the heart of the Advisory Selling Method. It is in this mode that a trusted advisor draws out the client's commitment to take an action unlike the selling agent who is trying to impose their ideas about what action the client should take. Eduction is a little used word and unfamiliar concept. Spell checkers will tell you that the word is misspelled and should be changed to education. This is because both the word "eduction" and the word "education" come from the Latin word Educo which means to draw out or bring out but they are not the same.

Even though most people are unaware that eduction exists, they have done it more often than they realize. Because they are not aware of it, they cannot replicate it. This lack of awareness causes selling agents to credit their normal selling techniques when they are successful. But this can never be the case because induction, deduction, reduction, and seduction are all counter to being a commitment-based advisor. It is the basic mission of the Advisory Selling Method to develop eductive skills.

77

Because we fail to see the underlying commitment-based eductive principles at work, we mistakenly believe that the agenda-based modes of influence are working in our favor. We end up pursuing the counterproductive modes more and more vigorously without producing expected results. This is why so many people view sales as hard to do.

In the classroom, most teachers educate rather than educe. They present information from the outside and work to push it inside the student's awareness in an effort to make them more brilliant. It's common for students to cram for tests, desperately trying to stuff as much information into their brains as possible in order to make the grade and get the gold star. Some students do not have the capacity to learn the information quick enough in the manner presented and fall short on the test or fail. This approach to education does not empower them, or bring out their true creative talent from within, because much of human creativity is not included within the limits set by the standards of normal education or the testing process. Teaching to the test does not teach every student in a manner consistent with what they need. Instead, it fosters failure.

Teachers are only able to create success for a small portion of students by pushing copious amounts of information at them, even when this strategy is well intended. Hoping to create brilliance by means of information overload is counterproductive to many students' ability to bring forth and apply their aptitude from the inside out. The result is that teachers produce a few successful students, while others lag because of this approach to education. The more concerning consequence is that the students who have fallen behind feel like losers in the game. They often become habitual failures and ultimately dropout. The students that do succeed have been able to educe their own brilliance. Our most memorable teachers likely knew how to find the balance between education and eduction to elevate student aptitude.

While teachers typically push information at students, coaches focus on bringing out each player's intrinsic brilliance from within. A coach may use some induction (threats), deduction (explanations), reduction (put-downs), and seduction (bribes), but the overriding skill of a coach is eduction, bringing out the stamina, courage, skill, and tenacity of a player in the face of significant challenges. The greatest coaches are adept at all five modes of influence, but they shine at eduction.

Selling agents who attempt to build rapport by cramming information about themselves, their track record, market knowledge, and company platform down a client's throat, fail to see that clients are not interested in the agent's capabilities. Clients are only interested in accomplishing what matters most to them. In Advisory Selling, agents shift from imposing their own solutions to bringing out the solutions from within the client. Rather than fixing a problem, which is the typical mode of interaction, in Advisory Selling, you learn to build on the accomplishments of your clients to inspire improvements in them that lead to new possibilities.

When selling agents become trusted advisors and shift their focus to eductive selling, it's much more likely that they will build successful client relationships that will empower those clients to experience the fulfillment of their project. The trick is to learn to do this with conscious intention so that the results are replicable. Eduction is a natural skill available to all of us.

What does the Eductive Mode of Influence look like in the real world? A parent or teacher can acknowledge a child's achievements, emphasizing what skills helped them become successful. They can then show that child or student how to use their own brilliance to access the next level of achievement. A manager can acknowledge good performance, encouraging the team to use those same skills to become leaders in their industry. A coach can deepen players' commitments by acknowledging and showcasing each player's unique skills in specific roles that benefit the entire team. A selling agent, as a trusted advisor, can encourage a client to set aside current perceptions and take action in a way that will further that client's best interest. An advisor does this by acknowledging a client's achievements while offering to help the client reach the next level in their project, profession, business, or enterprise.

Those who are at the top of their game have found a way to master the art of bringing forth winning characteristics from within a client. Many selling agents, however, position themselves center stage as the great performer. This forces clients to abdicate responsibility for the actions they must take, thereby transferring that responsibility onto the agent. When a deal works out, the client will claim credit. When a deal falls through, the agent gets the blame.

In Advisory Selling, the selling agent removes themself from the field, goes to the coaches' sideline, and pulls the client out of the stands onto the field. In doing so, the agent becomes an advisor who then gives the client the ball and helps them win their game. This is what clients want even though they claim that they want an agent to do it for them.

What You Can Do

I challenge you to recognize when you're operating from your normal agenda-based modes of influence and to make a conscious shift to using the more natural, commitment-based Eductive Mode of Influence. This is what the Advisory Selling Method helps you develop and apply. Each of these five modes of influence date back to prehistoric times. Each mode has served its purpose when employed. From cave dwellers to cowboys, from monarchies to family matriarchs, from CEOs to coaches, the exertion of influence has been the driving force of all human conversation. As we have already established, all human conversations are either agenda-based selling conversations or advisory conversations.

Agents who want to become trusted advisors can educe, draw out, their clients' projects and work with them to create a strategy for fulfilling that project. In this way, you create enduring partnerships with your clients. With partnership, deals transpire more smoothly, you are able to conduct more deals at the same time, and more deals close with greater certainty. All of this translates to more income. Advisors at this level know that when they are focused on having their clients win, they win as well. Only from this place can you and your client truly win every time.

We all have innate commitment-based inceptive selling skills that, once brought out, displace the dominance of our accumulated normal deceptive selling habits.

CHAPTER FIVE
BREAKING OUR SELLING HABITS
Shifting from Adversarial to Advisory Conversations

O ur first lesson in selling came with the first words we spoke. When we said our first words, our parents went crazy. They invited friends and family to hear us, and they went wild too. At that moment, it seemed that all we had to do was say a word or two, and we could get anything we wanted. For most of us this delusion lasted only until we were told to shut up. That's when our initial sense of selling suddenly got tougher.

Many of us continue to wonder why so many of our selling conversations just don't work. It's because the approaches we keep using are built from common adversarial habits that continue to work against us. Most adults think that if they are talking, they know what they are talking about, and they think that their words can get them what they want. Nothing could be further from the truth as our use of normal adversarial language can easily betray our best intentions. When the words we speak are automatic, and we do not choose them with intention, we cannot expect a desired outcome. Not only are we unconscious of the words we are using, we are blind to the impact of those words and how we use them on the recipient. We often set out to create an ally but end up developing an adversary.

Over the years, each of us has developed habits designed to get what we want from others to fulfill our own agendas. We often fail to see how much these habits work against us in our selling conversation and how they have made selling more difficult by not taking into account what the other person wanted or needed. We learned these behaviors from parents, teachers, managers, consultants, and many others. Sales trainers charge a boatload of money to teach us what we have already been taught many times over, further reinforcing these counterproductive habits as the ultimate selling skills to master.

Most of us aren't aware of what we are saying when we are speaking. We spew out our thoughts without considering how we are conveying information, how we are branding ourselves, or our impact on listeners. In this chapter, we will investigate how we speak our thoughts out loud and how our speech has been shaped by our many influential teachers. As we do this, you should listen to your own conversations and examine if what you are saying offers real value to your listeners. If you wake up to the reality of the impact of what's coming out of your mouth, and change your use of language, you get much better at selling.

Who We Are Talking To

Imagine a cartoon with two heads facing each other with a thought bubble over each head. Inside each bubble is each person's picture of what is happening when they are in conversation with the person in front of them. The question becomes, which person are we really speaking with, the one in front of us or the one we see in our head? More often than not, we are speaking to our picture of the client in our own bubble, not to the person in front of us. This is where communication breaks down. The seemingly great communication that is happening in the bubble in our head is different from what is happening in the bubble in the client's head. Because we believe what we are saying to another person is the same as what we are saying in our own head, we assume that we are being understood. Nothing could be further from the truth.

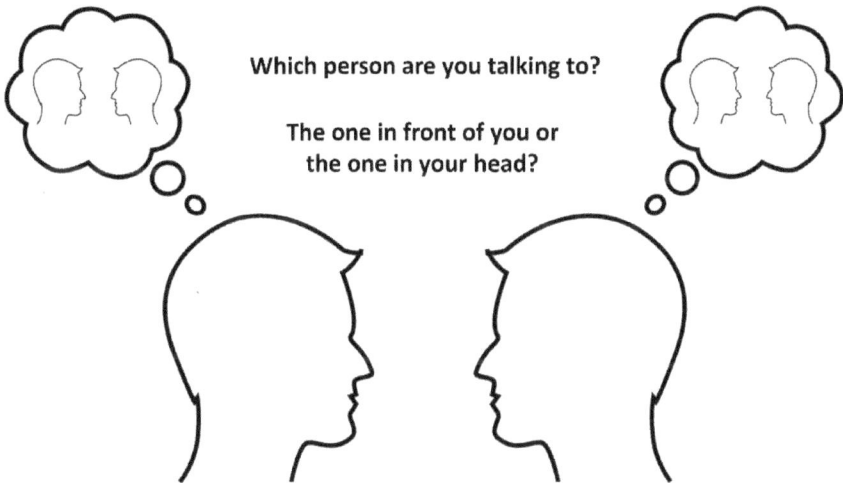

Which person are you talking to?

The one in front of you or
the one in your head?

Other people only hear what they think you are saying in their bubble. Therefore, each person has completely different ideas about what was said and will swear to you that what they were thinking is in fact what was stated. Even though we understand the thoughts in our bubble, we are often unable to translate those thoughts when we are speaking with another person. The intent of those thoughts never penetrates the other person's bubble, and vice versa. Because of this we never connect. Selling agents wonder why getting a deal done can be so difficult. This is the reason. Until this impediment to communication gets resolved, their selling process will be ineffective.

The first step to making a real connection with a client is to get out of our own bubble by realizing that the person who we think we see in front of us and what we think we heard them say may not be accurate. The second step is to get the client out of their bubble so they can hear what we are saying. This is where powerful questions come into play. This means that we cannot ask questions for which we think we already have the answers. Asking questions without any preconceived notions or expectations of the responses will yield new and valuable information that can be used to further connect with a client. We must practice the art of "not knowing" in order to discover things about the client that we don't know that we don't know.

Subjective reality is what people think and therefore "know" to be true, yet it only exists in their heads. These thoughts are the stories about the facts that we tell ourselves, and they are often inconsistent and disconnected from the objective world of measurable, observable facts. The good news is that we can help clients free themselves from being trapped by their own subjective reality where nothing new or useful can be created. Advisory Selling teaches us how to stay out of the subjective reality in our head and cut through the client's subjective reality that they've convinced themselves to be true.

Clients fall into delusion when they deny facts that they don't want to face, then deceive others about those facts and buy the lie as if it were real. This is what is meant by BS, the Big Story. We all have one. We have to learn how to break out of our own BS and help others do the same. In order to create something with the client, we must get both ourselves and them out of subjective reality and into objective reality where creativity can be accessed. Only then can the true definition of selling be fulfilled, which is to work with the client to create a vision of the future that's compelling enough to influence their actions in the present.

To that end, it's important to listen to what's coming out of your mouth because most of us are tone-deaf to what we are actually saying. We often have little clue about the impact of our words and even less sense of what the listener is hearing. When we speak, we expect certain actions and results to be produced. Yet, our expectations have no power, except to upset us when they are unfulfilled. To resolve this, we must "put our attention on our intention through inspection," paying attention to what we are saying, why we are saying it, and what the client is receiving. In the simplest of terms, this can be achieved by asking the client to reflect back to us what they heard before taking the next step.

Our default survival-driven language skills betray us again and again. We seldom see that the culprit is our own use of "normal" language learned from others who knew no better themselves. We must embrace the idea that we don't really know what we are saying, so we need to listen to our words and manage them appropriately. If we continue to ignore the real impact of what we're saying, we will never become adept at influencing others to take appropriate action that is based on truth.

Learned Adversarial Selling Habits

At each stage of "normal" learning, the next set of teachers takes over, sinking us deeper into a toxic culture of selling lies that is difficult to shake. When we learned the language of selling from our parents, teachers, managers, consultants, and sales trainers, we were exposed to the commonly used tactics and tricks unwittingly perpetuated by them in an invisible cycle which they had learned from their parents, which we then teach our children. Because our parents, as agents, are the biggest influencers in our lives and because they withhold information or say things that are untrue, we have been influenced to do the same. Agents think they are selling the truth but they are not. They don't do this on purpose; they can't help themselves because that is how they were taught. We have been conditioned to lie. Regardless of the role people play, these basic adversarial habits are the same, only the purpose is different. After years of being hammered by this mode of training, these habits became ingrained in our listening, speaking, thinking, and actions.

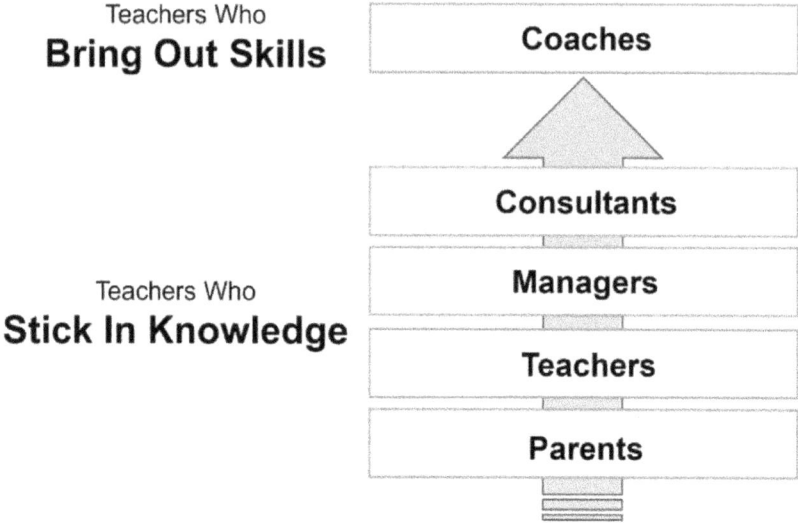

Teachers Who
Bring Out Skills

Coaches

Consultants

Teachers Who
Stick In Knowledge

Managers

Teachers

Parents

Once we learn from our parents, our teachers take over, teaching us the same habits, but from a different perspective. We choose a career pathway, we get hired, and our managers reinforce this same type of training in the context of our job and career. Sales consultants take it to yet another level. We hire them to teach us the same techniques learned from all our previous educators, further cementing these habits. By this time, we are convinced that the "great" techniques we've learned are working in our favor when, in truth, they are actually working against us. This makes selling much harder and a lot less fun.

There is another method of working with people that shifts from sticking in new information to bringing out the natural skills of a person and helping them put those skills to work. This is called coaching. Not only do coaches do everything the teacher does, but they also bring out the courage, stamina, and drive within all of us that is needed to win. The great teachers we all remember are the ones who were also eductive coaches who sold the truth of what could be achieved.

Let's take a deep dive into what we have learned in the context of the six sets of adversarial selling habits that are predominately taught to professional selling agents. These agenda-based selling tactics, tricks, techniques, triggers, and traps of traditional selling have become internalized habits used by everyone, frequently leading to terms of incarceration.

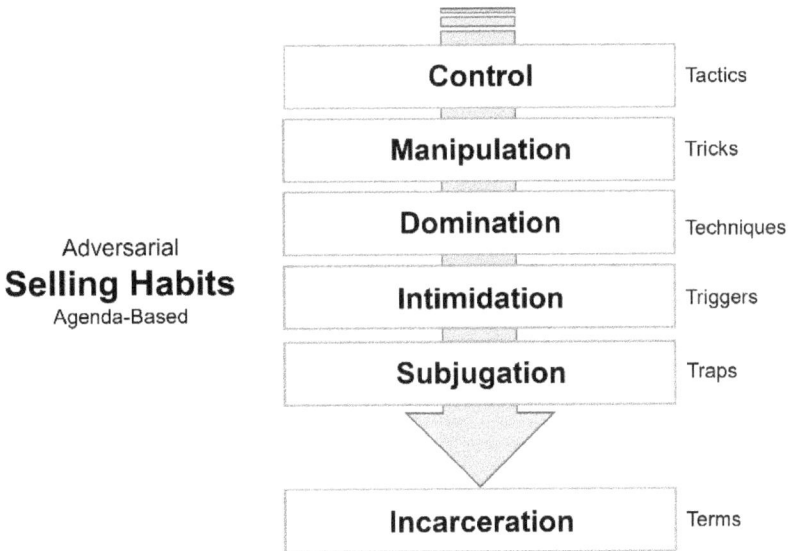

Adversarial **Selling Habits** Agenda-Based		
Control	Tactics
Manipulation	Tricks
Domination	Techniques
Intimidation	Triggers
Subjugation	Traps
Incarceration	Terms

These normal selling habits are the main fare at any sales training, despite the fact that trainers work hard to rebrand them with new names, implying a different result. The problem is that sales trainers have no clue about what they are teaching and the damage it can do. Control Tactics immediately push a client into an adversarial relationship with an agent. Manipulation Tricks sell lies that undermine trust. Domination Techniques force a client to submit or rebel. Intimidation

Triggers make clients want to run the other way. Subjugation Traps box clients in. And Incarceration Terms, that clients are desperate to escape, are the reason why so many agent-client relationships never endure. Once a client has been inappropriately sold by these agenda-based practices, the only way out is a lawsuit and that never empowers a client-agent partnership. Following is a list of ways that each of these adversarial habits are applied.

Control Tactics

- o Control the conversation
- o Overcome objections
- o Hit their hot buttons

Manipulation Tricks

- o Throw them a softening statement
- o Imply an impending event
- o Defer to a higher power

Domination Technique

- o Tell them how to think
- o Tell them what to do
- o Do a tie-down

Intimidation Triggers

- o Create urgency
- o Negative outcome
- o Artificial deadline

Subjugation Traps (Closing)

- o Do a take-away
- o Alternate choice trial close
- o Make them say thank you

Incarceration Terms

- o Agreement
- o Fees
- o Conditions

These approaches are the most touted in sales trainings and all of them are designed to lead to incarceration. If you have ever attended a sales training, whether independent or in-house, most of these techniques will be familiar. Once you become aware that these habits are habits, rather than being asleep to them, you then have a choice of whether to use them or not.Sales trainers have repackaged the habits we learned from our previous teachers into a routine that they claim are new. They are not. Once you become aware that these "new" habits are just your default habits, rather than being asleep to them, you wake up to the truth that everything you learned gets in the way of the natural selling process. Let's explore why.

Normal Adversarial Selling Conversations

Using what's been covered in previous chapters, we'll examine a normal adversarial selling conversation between an agent and a client. In Chapter 3, you learned about four agenda-based selling strategies (i.e., Aggressive, Aversive, Apathetic, Attentive) and in Chapter 4, you learned about four agenda-based modes of influence (i.e., Inductive, Deductive, Reductive, Seductive). When a selling agent has their financial or professional survival threatened, it is possible for them to hit every strategy and every mode of influence in the same conversation. The agenda easily becomes "get a deal so I can get a check so I can get my bills paid." When we step into the "get" mode, we become agenda-based and our deeply engrained inherited, acquired, and developed language habits take control of us such that what comes out of our mouth becomes highly adversarial.

Below is an example conversation that contains the fifteen well-established adversarial selling techniques commonly taught in most sales trainings and encouraged by most sales managers. The conversation has been kept generic so that you get the impact of the techniques and not caught up in the nuances of one industry or another. The two threads of common selling strategies and modes of influence are woven together around the tactics, triggers, techniques, tricks, and traps used in most selling conversations. As you follow what the agent is saying, you will see the names of the techniques, the strategy, and mode of influence so you see them all at work in the same conversation. The elements of a conversation may not always go in this order but, more often than not, they do.

In this instance the agent is speaking with their client about an opportunity that would result in a big paycheck for the agent but would be detrimental to the client. As the client comes to see the chance that the purchase might be a mistake, they grow more and more protective and determined to resist the agenda-based approach of the agent. When two agendas are not in alignment, the only outcome can be a battle to see who knows best, who will win, and who will lose. If you engage in an adversarial conversation with a client, you will see how clients will fight you to the point of complete destruction of the relationship. If anyone loses, everyone loses.

Control Tactics – Aggressive/Inductive

Tactic 1: Control the Conversation

Agent: Hi, good to see you. I was nearby and thought I'd pop in early so we'd have more time to meet. Let me start our talk with an overview of what I do so you understand what we're capable of providing and then we'll get into your situation.

Client: I'm not sure this is the best time to meet. I'd rather start at the time we set which is two hours from now.

Tactic 2: Overcome Objections

Agent: I got here early so we can jump right in. It seems I've double booked myself because we're so busy. Sorry about that but I know you can't afford to wait until I can get back here next week to get started on your financing.

Client: This is going to throw me off but let's see what we can do.

Tactic 3: Hit Their Hot Buttons

Agent: Just to remind you we're headed into challenging economic times, and you don't want your business to suddenly be put at risk. So, getting your financing underway as soon as possible is critical.

Client: True.

Manipulation Tricks – Aversive/Deductive

Trick 1: Throw Them a Softening Statement

Agent: I'm not trying to push you into doing anything and can work with you at your pace, but economic changes won't wait for you to get ready. We must go sooner than later.

Client: I understand.

Trick 2: Imply an Impending Event

> **Agent:** As you may have heard, the Fed is looking at more interest rate hikes this year, and you'll need to move quickly before that happens.

> **Client:** (Nods)

Trick 3: Defer to a Higher Power

> **Agent:** Our research department tells me that you're one of many in this situation. We need to beat the rush so you don't end up standing in line or missing out altogether.

> **Client:** Don't want that.

Domination Techniques – Apathetic/Reductive

Technique 1: Tell Them How to Think

> **Agent:** In order to help you, I'll need to put a lot of other clients on hold. What we're offering is a quick and simple solution. I can't afford to care about whether or not you get the financing you need.

> **Client:** I get it.

Technique 2: Tell Them What to Do

> **Agent:** You need to get things rolling, starting with completing the paperwork I asked for last week.

> **Client:** I don't have all the information from my accountant yet.

> **Agent:** Look, you have to get it together because others seem to have a lot better handle on their records. Tell your account-

ant he's putting you at risk and let's get started on the paperwork now. We can plug in the numbers when you get them.

Technique 3: Do a Tie-Down

Agent: Don't you agree?

Client: I'd rather know the numbers, but I guess we can get started.

Intimidation Triggers – Attentive/Seductive

Trigger 1: Create Urgency

Agent: I understand you're under pressure so I'm willing to waive some of the normal fees to make this easier for you. You'll need to make a firm commitment now or I can't promise you our help.

Client: I'd appreciate whatever you can do to help.

Trigger 2: Negative Outcome

Agent: If we fail to get this done you will miss the boat on interest rates and your business will feel the squeeze. That could make things very difficult.

Client: (looks concerned)

Trigger 3: Artificial Deadline

Agent: We should've started weeks ago and time is already slipping through our fingers.

Client: Oh, no!

Subjugation Traps (Closing) – Aggressive/Inductive

Trap 1: Do a Take-Away

> **Agent:** If you can't commit then we'll need to pull back and move on to others and let you ride this out yourself.
>
> **Client:** (silent)

Trap 2: Alternate Choice Trial Close

> **Agent:** I can offer you this. Either sign up today so we're locked in for our retainer agreement or I could come back on Monday which would give you a chance to get your numbers together.
>
> **Client:** Let's do Monday and I'll contact my accountant today.

Trap 3: Make Them Say Thank You

> **Agent:** When this is all done, you're gonna thank me.
>
> **Client:** I can start now. Thanks.

Incarceration Terms – Aversive/Deductive

Terms 1: Offer an Agreement

> **Agent:** Here's the agreement for you to sign and you can attach numbers from your account. I suggest you sign it now so we can get our team working on your behalf. You must understand, we have many complex steps to take just to get you in a position for financing and the sooner we get started the better it'll be for you.
>
> **Client:** Okay, where do I sign?

Terms 2: Specify the Duration

> **Agent:** The process should take about three months overall to find the right funding source and a viable deal for you. Our retainer is due the first of each month.

> **Client:** Are there any other obligations?

Terms 3: Minimize the Obligations

> **Agent:** Nothing much to worry about, all standard stuff. I'll take your agreement and get things rolling today. Get those numbers by Monday so I can keep things moving with my team rather than coming back.

> **Client:** I'll get on it.

None of these often-used techniques will cultivate a deeper agent-client partnership. The likely outcome is that the client will do what is recommended for a few days, then rebel, and go back to doing what they've always done. This is because this selling conversation is all about what the agent wants. No questions were asked. There's no consideration of what the client wants or is committed to doing because the client is given no opportunity to generate their commitment. They are simply told what to do. Many selling agents approach clients in much the same way.

For many of you, much of this will sound familiar. Obviously, we learned these techniques from listening to our many educators along the way. Surely by now, they are so ingrained that you will never part with them. If, however, you want to manage and ultimately minimize the use of them, you must first pay attention to the words pouring from your mouth. These deeply embedded speaking habits can make every selling conversation competitive, rather than collaborative. This also means that the conversations will be more difficult to deliver, and less likely to result in success, because it causes a lot more work for the same limited results.

A Not So Common Advisory Conversation

In respect to the ASM, the success of any client conversation relies on three critical practices: evoking rapport, generating projects, and forging partnership. These advisory selling language skills are explored in detail in Chapter 8 and they play a pivotal role in building a strong foundation for a productive and enduring relationship between the advisor and the client.

What makes the Advisory Selling Method so powerful is the underlying Modular Learning Architecture. This approach to conversation design comes from the pre-print era when teaching occurred in the form of story-telling. The Advisory Selling Method utilizes key components of oral tradition: systematic repetition, alliteration, and coding. It's important to understand that there is a structure to the language used in ASM.

Many people search for the best words to use, only to be looking in all the wrong places. Regardless of your content, your message cannot be effectively delivered without the right structure, or language architecture. Each of the six ASM modules contains three practices that work together to accomplish a result. Understanding how the modules are built, the role of each practice, and how they work together to produce results in conversation will give you full access to the power of the method. The modular language architecture embodied in this approach makes learning deeper and more permanent. This is how it works.

Module 1	Practice 1	**Evoking Rapport**	Generator
Building Partnerships	Practice 2	**Generating Projects**	Operator
	Practice 3	**Forging Partnership**	Regulator

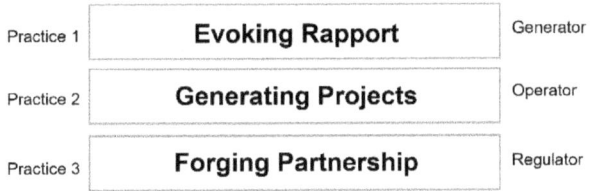

As indicated, Practice 1 is the Generator. It generates the direction and energy of the module. Practice 2 is the Operator and is the workhorse practice of the module. Practice 3 is the Regulator because this practice keeps the conversation on track to produce the end result called partnership.

Within each Practice there are five steps and each performs a specific function for accomplishing the purpose of the practice which, in turn, empowers the other practices within the module.

	Step 1	**Opening**	Lead
	Step 2	**Permission**	Ground
Practice 1	Step 3	**Interest**	Key
Evoking Rapport	Step 4	**Detachment**	Offer
	Step 5	**Questions**	Transition

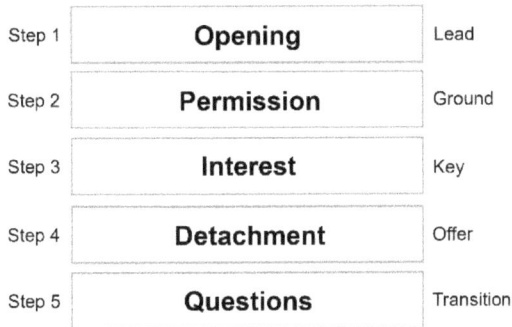

The Lead function is Opening (Step 1) and establishes the direction of the practice, stepping up to the door of rapport. The Ground function, Permission (Step 2), brings the conversation down to earth and knocks on the door of rapport. The Key function is Interest (Step 3). It unlocks the door to rapport. The Offer function, Detachment (Step 4), makes an offer because selling is making offers and getting them accepted, thereby opening the door to rapport. The last function,

Transition, is Questions (Step 5). This allows you to step through the door to rapport and into the next practice.

As mentioned, each module of the ASM is comprised of three practices, each with five steps that perform a specific function. The practices, steps, and functions are listed below for the first module, Building Partnership.

Evoking Rapport

- o   Opening (Lead)
- o   Permission (Ground)
- o   Interest (Key)
- o   Detachment (Offer)
- o   Questions (Transition)

Generating Projects

- o   History (Lead)
- o   Facts (Ground)
- o   Accomplished (Key)
- o   Needed (Offer)
- o   Possible (Transition)

Forging Partnership

- o   Risks (Lead)
- o   Responsibility (Ground)
- o   Declaration (Key
- o   Invitation (Offer)
- o   Promise (Transition)

Establishing rapport creates a meaningful connection with the client by opening their protective listening. Protective listening is always automatically present in every conversation and must be dealt with.

The client is not going to be authentic about their wants and needs until receptive listening is present. When the client senses the agent's genuine interest and feels heard, they begin to see the agent as a trusted advisor.

Generating projects uses the evoking rapport practice to open the doorway to exploring with the client the three components of their project – where they are now, where they want to go, and how they are going to get there. In order to clarify the project, it is important to ask "why-based" questions that draw out the client's unique concerns. As the advisor gains deeper insights into the client's objectives and challenges, they can propose actionable options that will position the client to make an appropriate choice that helps them fulfill their desired project.

Ultimately, Advisory Selling goes beyond a mere transaction, it is the pathway to building a long-term partnership. By forging partnership, the client becomes committed to their project. The agent becomes equally invested in the client's success, fostering a sense of shared responsibility for achieving desired outcomes.

This module offers a set of natural language skills for building enduring partnerships with colleagues and clients. These practices, with each of their five steps, are demonstrated in the following advisor and client conversation. They are not a new set of tricks nor are they the normal agenda-based habits we mentioned earlier. These are commitment-based steps that bring out your innate skills so you naturally connect with clients as they shift from being protective in how they listen to being more receptive.

An advisory conversation offers a different experience for the client and opens the doorway to long-term partnership. The following example embodies the heart of Advisory Selling. Take note of the difference in the flow and feel of this conversation. Each step, with its unique function, naturally draws the conversation forward. Advisors must use an authentic selling strategy and practice the eductive mode of influence. If you follow along carefully you will see the functions of each of the practices and steps. They follow the natural course that leads to partnership, virtually every time. They can even be applied in the same conversation with the same person a number of times yet the steps at work are never noticed. This is because they are not a new set of tricks but the application of natural skills we all have.

Advisor & Client Conversation

Practice 1: Evoke Rapport - Generator

Step 1: Opening (Lead)

> **Advisor:** We have been speaking with numerous clients in your area and have learned a lot from these conversations, but we don't know you yet. We have some ideas about where your market's headed that we look forward to sharing with you.
>
> **Client:** Good to meet you.

Step 2: Permission (Ground)

> **Advisor:** If it's okay with you, let's take whatever time is necessary to give us a chance to take a deep dive into your situation and put some bold new ideas on the table that you may not yet have considered.
>
> **Client:** Sounds good.

Step 3: Interest (Key)

> **Advisor:** It is important to us that you know our interest is in

you, what relationship we can build, and being part of your success in the future.

Client: Understood.

Step 4: Detachment (Offer)

>**Advisor:** Also whether or not we work together now or in the future, here is what we are offering. We're offering to look at your situation in detail and explore how other clients are dealing with similar concerns.

>**Client:** We're doing fine but higher interest rates on financing will delay our ability to make it profitable.

>**Advisor:** Then we'll take what we learn from you today and put together our analysis of your financial situation and the options that'll be available to you at this time so you can make the best possible choice as to how to go forward.

>**Client:** Great!

Step 5: Questions (Transition)

>**Advisor:** I sent you three preparation questions to think about in my email confirming this meeting. Did you have a chance to think about them?

>**Client:** I saw them but haven't had a chance to spend much time thinking about them.

>**Advisor:** Let's take a look at them now starting with my first question. What do you feel you have accomplished so far with your business?

Practice 2: Generate Projects – Operator

Step 1: History (Lead)

> **Client:** We've accomplished quite a bit, I think.
>
> **Advisor:** Tell me why you say that.
>
> **Client:** We got through the last downturn after launching our first project and its in a strong position so far. Now we're headed into another time of economic changes and our ability to do it again is at risk. With interest rates the way they are any chance of financing gets us behind the eight-ball from the get-go.

Step 2: Facts (Ground)

> **Advisor:** Can you give me more details of what you did to finance your first project and what you see the challenges are now?
>
> **Client:** Our first project got started before the last downturn so we were in a strong position with solid financing. Now we have an even bigger game we want to launch but interest rates could crush our profitability to almost nothing for a few years or so.

Step 3: Accomplished (Key)

> **Advisor:** Well, it's clear to me that you have accomplished a lot so far and that you have a good foundation to build on.
>
> **Client:** Yeah, but we're not sure how to go forward.

Step 4: Needed (Offer)

> **Advisor:** That's why we're here as advisors to guide you through the process of identifying a variety of funding sources

and then putting together our strategic analysis of your situation so you can see the options available to you at this time. This will put you in a position to make some smart choices in the face of the challenges with the economy.

Client: I'm on board.

Agent: We'll need this list of financial records to do our work. How soon can you gather this information?

Client: We already have it because you mentioned in your email that for speedy service we should have it ready for you today.

Step 5: Possible (Transition)

Advisor: Great! Now may I ask, once we get this done, what do you see as possible for you and the project you're looking to launch?

Client: What's possible for us is to dramatically expand our business and, via social media and some AI, deliver to more people than ever before. That would put us in a whole new category of business and keep us at that level for years to come.

Practice 3: Forging Partnership – Regulator

Step 1: Risks (Lead)

Advisor: I can see you've got a compelling future and we're looking forward to helping you make that happen. It's important to remember that, given a lot of factors such as economic changes and global challenges, there are risks that come with an expansion at this time. But that's why we are here, to help you face those risks effectively.

Client: Appreciated.

Step 2: Responsibility (Ground)

> **Advisor:** You'll need to take responsibility for working closely with us each step of the way which means being available for communication with us regularly. Failure to do so means we might have an opportunity for you and you could miss out on it. We'll be responsible for ensuring that you are fully up to speed at all times with the actions we are taking.

> **Client:** Good for me.

Step 3: Declaration (Key)

> **Advisor:** We know you can do this and are totally committed to helping you get this done.

> **Client:** Thanks.

Step 4: Invitation (Offer)

> **Advisor:** We invite you to make a commitment today to move forward with us and finalize our agreement so that our team can be set in motion on your behalf and you can start thinking about your next steps.

> **Client:** I accept.

Step 5: Promise (Transition)

> **Advisor:** Our promise is that you'll have complete clarity each step of the way and can have certainty that you'll be making the right choices at the right time.

> **Client:** I couldn't ask for more than that.

But, in order to learn the method, we must make sure you understand how the method is built because how it is built is the most important part of why the method works so well.

What You Can Do

What type of selling conversation will be required to serve another person's best interest? The answer is always an Advisory Selling conversation. Having taken the first step of becoming aware of how often you use normal selling techniques, you better understand how your work with the Advisory Selling Method will make a difference in how you connect with clients. You discover how you can reduce your dependency on counterproductive, highly manipulative adversarial techniques.

One of the ways you can displace these habits is to practice the art of not knowing. This positions you to ask powerful questions. Stop looking for what you need to fulfill your agenda and start listening to what the client needs to empower them to achieve what they want. When you really listen to what the client is actually saying, versus what you perceive they are saying, you are able to push aside your agenda-based approach which has been shaping what you are able to hear and not hear. But in order to learn the method we must make sure you understand how the method is built because how it is built is the most important part of why the method works so well.

As you practice the Advisory Selling Method, your natural skills will begin to displace your common adversarial ingrained habits. Instead, they can be integrated into your Advisory Selling conversations in a way that will forward your partnership with a client in pursuit of their project. Since you can never fully get rid of them, you must learn how to best use them.

With nearly eight billion people on the planet,
the overwhelming challenge is getting heard.

CHAPTER SIX
NAVIGATING THE SEA OF BABBLE
Charting Your Course to a New Way of Selling

With almost eight billion people on Earth, a tsunami of conversations washes across the planet 24/7. We are swimming in a vast "ocean" of talk made up of selling conversations. When we add print, media, and the Internet, this wave multiplies many times in size. I call this the Sea of Babble.

This treacherous wave pitches people to the very top and then crashes them back to the bottom. Since the Sea of Babble is mostly filled with normal selling conversations made up of the common adversarial selling tactics, tricks, and techniques, we must swim in this sea of lies at great risk. In this sink or swim world, only a few keep their heads above water and get their voices heard. Many give up and end up being tossed by the waves and shifting tides. How can you navigate this sea? Advisory Selling teaches you how to sell the truth so you can cut through these waters with greater certainty and success.

Few voices ever rise above the din created by the crashing waves in the Sea of Babble. And even when they do, they are usually audible for only a fleeting moment. Getting heard by others is a daunting challenge. As an agent, getting heard by clients, whether individually or as part of a larger audience, is an even bigger one. A hundred outreach phone calls may produce only one or two good conversations and a lot of brush offs and hang ups. The shape of these many conversations is a prime determinant of the quality of the world we inhabit.

Advisory Selling is the only way to effectively navigate the Sea of Babble and interact with others as we swim through it, helping our message rise above the noise. Without it, you might as well hang onto your lifeboat and see where the storms take you. You might get lucky, but most don't. The Advisory Selling approach is easier to manage, and more empowering than any approach you've used in the past.

Taking On a New Way of Selling

The Advisory Selling Method will put an engine with a tiller on your lifeboat so you can steer yourself somewhere meaningful and not resign yourself to wherever the currents take you. Because this new selling approach rises above the normal transactional approach, it ensures that you connect with colleagues, clients, and customers on the "human side" of the selling equation. Drawing out these innate skills will help you overcome what I call protective listening, as demonstrated by the many clients who hang up on you, brush you off, or put you down.

We all have a high degree of automatic listening because we all need to protect ourselves from the onslaught of the Sea of Babble. Clients defensively narrow the channel by which they allow information to penetrate their world. Another way to envision this is to make a fist, hold it up to your eye, and make a small hole to look through. You won't see much at all. This first line of defense is what selling agents face whenever they make a call. We rarely pick up an unknown incoming call or, as soon as we hear the buzz of a call center or a generic "Congratulations!" we hang up immediately. Like our clients we must protect ourselves from the onslaught of adversarial selling conversations that come at us every day, all day, in every way.

We have a clear choice between trying to outsmart clients by selling lies or working with them in full partnership selling the truth. By working in partnership with clients and helping them make appropriate choices, you are better able to turn their protective listening into receptive listening and, therefore, results.

Five Common Ways of Adversarial Selling

To better understand the choices we have when dealing with the Sea of Babble, let's explore the types of selling that shape our conversations. These are either agenda-based normal selling conversations or commitment-based Advisory Selling conversations. Selling agents use the common agenda-based selling techniques to reduce the risks that accompany selling so they can navigate the Sea of Babble with some level of effectiveness. Advisory Selling will help you approach the challenges of selling head-on with real power and certainty once you are willing to give up the five common ways of selling and learn the Advisory Selling Method. To do so will require a significant leap into a new reality of selling. And staying in that new reality will require diligent practice.

An Uncommon
Way of Selling

Advisory Selling

Collaborative Selling
Consultative Selling

Five Common
Ways of Selling

Contract Selling
Competitive Selling
Conspiratorial Selling

Before we explore these five common ways of selling and the one uncommon way in more detail, let's review the definition of selling. Selling is "working with clients to create a vision of a future possibility that is compelling enough to change their actions in the present." The following six sections will show how this core principle is applied in very different ways. The results produced by these six ways of selling are on a spectrum. Deceptive selling is at one extreme and inceptive selling is at the other.

Conspiratorial Selling

The first common way of selling is Conspiratorial Selling, and it is located at the very end of the deceptive agenda-based selling side of the spectrum. It is the preferred method of any spammer looking to get money out of your bank account. This approach is used by some commodities brokers who deal in precious metals. This method intends to harm customers for the benefit of the agent and their company. This is the most ancient form of selling.

When selling is defined by human nature the laws of Mother Nature (competition, conspiracy, and conflict) rule and shape our deceptive selling conversations. Conspiratorial Selling is aimed at deceiving people and stealing money from them in any way possible. There are elements of this type of selling in everyone; no one is off the hook. But certain selling organizations plan out and practice how they will outright rip off unsuspecting people. In the face of this type of selling, the client never wins and, in the end, neither does the agent. We have all been on the receiving end and felt the sting of being duped at some point.

As an example, at the height of a financial crisis, fear can drive investors to call a gold trader, looking to gold to protect their capital. Some traders are ready to capitalize on such fear. A new selling agent could unknowingly be engaging in conspiratorial selling when he takes incoming calls from potential customers, assuring them that they are in the right place and in good hands. In the middle of what seems like a productive conversation, the young selling agent then passes the phone off to his senior selling agent, as he's been trained to do. The senior agent changes the tone of the conversation and begins to deepen the customer's alarm about the economy and promotes the idea that gold is a safe haven, knowing that he can use the unwitting customer's fear to his advantage. The senior agent minimizes the risks while reassuring their prospect that they have come to the right place. He pushes for a bigger investment, even if it means that the customer has to take out a line of credit to pay for it. The potential for loss for the client increases the more the senior agent talks and the client is likely to finish this process deep in debt. These traders are not unlike terrorists in their approach.

Selling is our primary means of survival as a species, and deceptive selling has been in our DNA for eons. Part of survival is predatory behavior, as in the gold example. Deception is an inevitable component of every selling conversation, and in these conspiratorial conversations, it is the only component. When we want them to be acceptable, we call our deceptions "little white lies."

Every industry has selling agents who look at customers only as idiots, suckers, and easy marks to be taken advantage of. Some of the best examples of deceptive selling can be found in TV advertising. In one ad, a woman pushes a pill across the table to her friend who's been sidelined by depression. The friend takes the pill, and her depression lifts. Suddenly she's going scuba diving and teaching her daughter to ride a bike. The pill doesn't assure any of this, but its projected vision of the future often compels customers to purchase the pill, even when they don't need it.

Conspiratorial Selling happens when a selling agent purposefully lies to take advantage of a customer, with no regard to the consequences for the customer. Some seek to harm the customer, rip them off, and then have a good laugh over drinks. Such an agent provides the least amount of service to extract the most money possible without heed to the amount of damage they are causing. Many Conspiratorial Selling agents see sales as a game where there are no fixed rules which they coyly play with a nod and a wink to each other.

Competitive Selling

In Competitive Selling, the most common type of agenda-based selling, agents and customers enter into an adversarial relationship to see who can outsmart the other. For selling agents, this approach to selling becomes an exhausting, debilitating grind because, in the end, the client always wins. Selling agents employing this approach play off clients' weaknesses to get their way. Their aim is to get the client's payment thereby "making the sale." They aren't stealing; they're simply out to get paid before hooking the next fish. These agents resort to the outright domination of customers. This means their pool of customers is only made up of those who are easily controlled.

Competitive Selling was most dominant in the 1990s and early 2000s. It was used in trading investments, most notably limited partnerships in the oil and gas industry. Some executives stole investors' money, claiming that it had paid for land rights, equipment, or labor, but that the wells did not pan out. The truth was that the money never went into the ground. It only went into the executives' pockets.

Competitive Selling is a brutal method, involving competition, conspiracy, and conflict, all of which lead to corruption. It's based on these basic principles of our human nature. This approach inevitably leads to everyone losing. In Competitive Selling, agents convince customers to act in the best interest of the agent, even when this comes at the customer's expense.

Let's consider a business owner who wanted to upgrade his copy machine so he could build workbooks that customers could order online. He was visited by a copy machine salesman who seemed interested in helping him get to the next level of machine. The agent spoke for some time about the features of a new machine and how it would give the customer the ability to print on a larger scale than his current copier. He even offered to throw in a free video camera once the sale was complete. The agent's answers to the customer's questions were spoken with great certainty, but not a lot of honesty. He promised that all of the things the customer could currently do with his small machine could be done more efficiently with a very expensive and larger machine.

It was a big investment for the customer, but he was determined to take his business to a new level. The customer was moving across the country and the sales agent he chose to work with offered to have the machine shipped to the new location and to take the old machine off the customer's hands. The main feature the customer needed was high-volume color printing. When the machine arrived at the new location, another company installed the machine. Although it printed in color and delivered higher volume, it was of poor color quality and at a slower speed. When the customer called the copy machine company, they told him that his contract could not be rescinded, but that his video camera was on the way. This customer never launched the new phase of his business and spent the next few years paying off the more expensive machine, justifying that at least it had been a good tax write-off.

Customers have learned the tricks of the selling agents, which the agents learned in their sales training, and use the same techniques on the agents. Thus, the natural process of selling is undermined. In this mode of selling, the agent rarely wins. Selling agents soon find themselves at the mercy of their customers' whims. They are used, abused, and then excused when they are no longer useful. In these scenarios, agents become a mere convenience rather than a respected asset to be called upon for advice.

Competitive Selling agents are forced to chase down customers just to pay their own bills, put food on their table, and look good to their bosses. Many agents fall into the trap of selling to survive. They become slaves to customers and companies. Forced into servitude by their firms' demands, these agents cater to their customers. Competitive Selling is not a lot of fun. There is little fulfillment and, inevitably, the results are poor.

Contract Selling

While conspiratorial agenda-based selling involves fooling customers into taking a risky action and competitive selling is about outsmarting customers to make a sale and get a check, Contract Selling takes competition, conspiracy, and conflict to a whole new level and can easily become corrupt. Contract Selling is about corralling customers into some agreement which they are obligated to fulfill unless they are willing to suffer the clearly spelled out consequences. Contract Selling inevitably leads to unpleasant surprises and many unfulfilled expectations for the customer. The selling agent also pays a heavy price and is never off the hook. Once a contract is signed, the customer is trapped into complying with the terms of the agreement even when it does not work in their favor and the agent inevitably loses an enduring customer relationship.

For example, a customer may be led to imagine the benefit that will pass to their family members once they are deceased, but the descendants do not receive everything that was promised. A customer who purchases a service agreement may have a picture of being rescued at the side of the road when their car breaks down, but later learns the limits of what the agreement covers. In an attempt to create security as they age, a person may buy a health and disability insurance policy without understanding the fine print regarding coverage. In each of these cases, the customer may not be protected to the extent that they were led to believe. They are still obligated to adhere to the strict terms of the contract and pay a premium for something that they may never receive. Customers are sold a vision of a future possibility that they may never experience and yet they must pay the premium month after month, chasing an imaginary outcome. In Contract Selling, the vision is emphasized, and the terms are minimized.

This type of selling can be inductive, deductive, reductive, seductive, or a combination of them all. The process is inductive when the selling agent is selling the idea of protection and security in the event of a possible catastrophe. It can be excruciatingly deductive if the agent outlines the terms of the contract in grueling detail, wearing the client down. When the customer is offered a less expensive option then is shamed into purchasing a more expensive version, Contract Selling becomes reductive. Lastly, Contract Selling is inevitably seductive, due to the many special offers that are emphasized to cloud the customer's view of what the terms of the contract will require.

Contract Selling goes beyond Conspiratorial and Competitive Selling in terms of offering intangible customer benefit. The potential benefits come at the cost of multi-year contractual incarceration within an agreement. Contract selling agents must continuously search for new victims and draw them into their trap. When these agents know that they are trapping people in an agreement with little or no benefit, and keep doing it again and again, they have become corrupt. They know they are potentially hurting people, yet in order to survive, they continue doing so. To justify their corruption, they need to build a Big Story about how customers are equally corrupt. These selling agents tell themselves they have every right to take advantage of such people.

Not all agreements are bad; some agents deliver excellent service. But when that isn't the case, it usually takes a lot of convincing, cajoling, corralling, and confusing to get customers to sign the agreement despite the costs. When the expectations of the customer cannot be fulfilled, problems arise. This means agony for the customer and annoyance for the selling agent. Since the agreement has been signed, and there is no way out for the customer, the only remaining option for the customer is an expensive lawsuit. When customers lose such a lawsuit, not only do they still have to pay the contracted premium, they must also pay the attorney fee for a case that they lost.

Consultative Selling

As selling agents grew weary of competing with conspiratorial customers to see who could get one up on the other and of the enslavement by demanding employers (exploiters), a new form of selling developed. This is called Consultative Selling. It emerged in the 1990s and has since gained significant traction. Today, it is the dominant way of selling employed by agents and endorsed by companies. This type of selling is a giant leap forward because, by focusing on solving client problems instead of putting agents' needs first, agents and companies have made a lot more money.

Although Consultative Selling is more "client-centric," it focuses on solving a problem, even if the client does not have one, and easily becomes agenda-based. Much like a pharmaceutical salesperson with a pill to sell, agents in this mode are looking for anything that appears to be a problem that their solution can supposedly remedy. This is the job of any consultant. They work hard to convince the customer to buy the product whether they truly need it or not, all so that the selling agent can get a check.

Consultants are hired to solve problems because of their experience and expertise. The consultative selling agent sells solutions. With Consultative Selling, customers become more like clients. These clients are the agent's center of attention which is a big improvement over Competitive and Conspiratorial Selling. In Consultative Selling, serving the client's best interest is now one of the priorities. There may still be some deception, but it is typically directed at helping a client make the best decision to solve their problem. The job of the agent becomes selling the client on having a problem in the first place so the agent can then sell them the solution that the agent is peddling. Some call this approach "Solution Selling." As we will see, although this is often claimed to be in the client's favor, it frequently is not.

The consultative approach takes many forms to sell solutions, but the best known is that of "Spin Selling." Selling agents who spin sell are focused on solving client problems. The acronym "SPIN" starts with "S" for *situation*. The consulting selling agent must first understand a client's situation. "P" is for *problem*. When an agent can't find a problem, they need to create one that matches the solution they are selling. Once the agent has defined the problem, "I" stands for the problem's *implications*. The agent defines the potential areas of concern before explaining "N," or the *need* the problem creates.

After defining the problem and identifying the possible implications of leaving it unsolved, the agent then showcases the payoffs inherent in the selling agent's solution. Once the selling agent has done this, the next challenge is to convince the client to buy into that solution. SPIN should, in fact, be "SPINS" to include the *solution* that the agent is selling. This kind of consultative relationship can easily revert to a competitive or conspiratorial relationship, depending on the survival-driven needs of the agent or the survival-driven priorities of the company they represent.

It's a lot of hard work and the result is usually uncertain and unsatisfying, even when the sale goes through. Furthermore, all the positioning, posturing, proving, and pretending designed to hide the agent's agenda can easily become exposed by a savvy client. Once the agent describes a solution, the client might agree with it then hire someone else to implement it or do it themselves. When these things happen, the roles get flipped, with the client using the adversarial tricks that they've learned from agents over the years, against the consulting agent who ends up a loser at his own game.

When the customer becomes a client whom the selling agent must please, Consultative Selling becomes its own grind. For example, an agent selling a technology solution delivers, at the request of the client, five complex presentations over eighteen months. His work is impeccable, and his presentations are spot-on. The client leads him to believe that he has the contract in the bag, then decides to go with a firm run by the brother of a friend. This selling agent has nothing to show for all his work and money spent even though he exceeded expectations.

When a selling agent repeatedly endures this difficult process, the job of selling becomes debilitating, expensive, and even self-destructive. Consultative Selling can become a competitive selling approach because so many other consultative agents are ready to compete with their own solutions. When several agents court the same prospective client, that client has all the power and can often force the winning agent into a condition of servitude in which they compromise their compensation and dignity. This is especially true of difficult clients who feel they are entitled to royal treatment and take great joy in taking advantage of agents.

Collaborative Selling

The next step beyond Consultative Selling is Collaborative Selling. This often takes the form of account-representation selling. In this form of selling, agents and clients forge an agreement to work together, but it can still be highly agenda-based. Usually, the agent has developed many of their natural skills and is able to connect with clients in a meaningful way so that the client only wants to work with that agent. Both selling agent and client work to ensure that the best interest of the other is an essential result. This is the ideal view of a collaborative selling relationship.

The downside of Collaborative Selling, much like Consultative Selling, is that the selling agent may become a servant to the client who then assumes a superior posture. In this case, the agent is entrapped by the client into a form of servitude and the agent cannot rebel without putting their ability to pay their own bills at risk. In many instances, to survive, the agent is required to make and keep commitments to a client who rarely does the same. The collaboration devolves into exploitation. Agents who feel exploited will eventually give clients only the minimum acceptable effort. Clients are left feeling that they have been ripped off because of their sense of entitlement. In spite of their agreement, this is no longer a collaborative relationship and both agent and client are left disempowered.

When a partnership, team, or entire organization works together rather than against each other, the awesome power of collaboration is unleashed. Only then can so much more be accomplished than what individuals could ever do on their own. It is because of our natural ability to collaborate that the human world exists at all. Achieving this level of collaboration happens for some very senior agents who have been able to stick it out for a decade or two, long enough for them to happen upon their natural collaborative skills and develop their ability to inspire clients. This can be a long, hard road, and frankly, most who begin that journey never make it to the end.

Selling is tough because most selling agents are using the adversarial selling techniques they learned in their sales training which results in failed attempts to forge a collaborative partnership with clients. Many agents bemoan that they have not fulfilled their aspirations for a better life as a result of their selling career. They are entangled in a daily battle of convincing customers and clients to do the "right thing" in order for the agents to get paid.

It is only after many years of failing yet persisting that a senior agent learns to drop their adversarial approach and allow their natural selling skills to emerge. For newer agents, from more recent generations, this is a dauntingly long, slow, and unexciting road. There is a way to get to that end much sooner, with less grief, and in a manner that is both fulfilling and fun. That way is Advisory Selling. To make agent-client collaboration possible, it is essential to bring out and develop these collaborative skills which we all have within us.

Advisory Selling

Advisory Selling is different from the previous five common ways of selling because it puts the client's best interest ahead of all other priorities. If a productive selling relationship is in the cards, the Advisory Selling Method is the most effective and most high-velocity way to get there. Your engagement with the Advisory Selling Method will change how you listen to others, how you speak to others, how you think about others, and who you become for them.

By following the Advisory Selling Method, you will significantly accelerate your ability to maximize your performance. However, there is a price tag. You must be willing to give up who you think you are to become a more authentic version of yourself. We all say that we want to be better, but that is a daunting challenge. When we don't live up to the promised newer better version of ourselves, we resort to playing the victim, blaming someone or something else for our failure and scrambling for the next new technique. This never gets us to where we say we want to be because we don't stick with that one either. The answer to this dilemma lies within. The truth is that you already have inside you everything you need to meet this challenge. Advisory Selling is the means by which you begin to loosen the stranglehold of all the tricks, tactics, and techniques you've relied on until now and allow the person you were meant to be to emerge. Your authentic self shows up.

In Advisory Selling, you are a trusted advisor. Being a trusted advisor is different from being a solution-selling consultant. The job of a consultant is to come up with answers to a problem. The advisor's job is to ask the questions that empower a client to come up with their own solutions in accord with what they truly want. Certain events, such as getting into school, getting a job, getting promoted, or getting married, are important enough that they call forth these natural skills. Because we have all already used them, we know that we already have them within us. The challenge is uncovering these skills from beneath the many layers of techniques and tricks used to influence the actions of others. Our natural skills are at work all the time, but we cannot always call upon them because we have not learned to see them for what they are when they appear.

Embracing A New Method

Advisory Selling, if you are to take it on, means to embrace a whole new way of selling. To do this you must have a process for installing something new that can effectively displace your deeply rooted normal ways of selling.

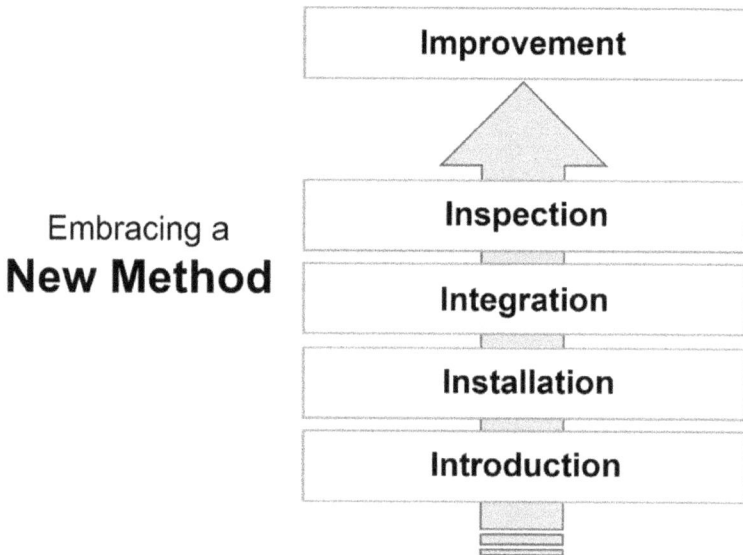

Embracing a
New Method

Improvement
Inspection
Integration
Installation
Introduction

Introduction

The simple act of being willing to be open to new ways of thinking is a line of demarcation from which there can be no return. Once you are introduced to new ways of doing things that contradict well-established habits, you are thrust into a turbulent mindset. Old thoughts and behaviors battle to maintain their hold. The more you resist the longer it will take and more painful the process will be. When you know something can be done differently, it will continue to gnaw at you until you make the change.

Installation

As you begin to take on the challenge of making the changes, you need to make the time to install the new method and displace the old. Your default ways of doing things are not going anywhere. Because they cannot be eradicated, the changes you make must work together with your old habits in such a way that your natural skills are free to blossom and become more dominant.

Simply learning about how to do something new is not enough. It requires the memorization of a new method so it becomes more naturally available as you engage in conversations with others. Systems for real learning need to be installed. These systems are continuous practice, interaction with others, welcoming guidance from those who have already made the changes, and being willing to fail often and persist over time.

Integration

It is one thing to install a new way of doing things and yet another to ensure that any new way is fully integrated. Without integration, your new approach to selling will be attacked by everything else that you are accustomed to doing in other areas of your life. The change you are attempting to make will ultimately be squeezed out causing you to revert back to old and familiar ways.

Integration means that old and new are now working together so that both can flourish rather than continuously battle for dominance. Once integration has been achieved, you can rest assured that your new way of doing things will continue to get stronger through practice and implementation.

Inspection

To ensure the continued growth of your new approach you must commit to a system of regular inspection to measure how often you revert to your old ways of doing things, how well your new ways are being executed, and what new possibilities can emerge if you continue the process. Inspection means stopping, honestly looking at what is happening, and being open to making corrections. This includes the input of others who are aligned with this new way of thinking. In these moments you have the opportunity to develop your skills into a new level of performance.

Improvement

As you inspect you will see improvements that can be integrated and that will ensure your new way will continue to flourish. Champions are always looking for opportunities for continuous improvement of their skills. This means that there can be no arrival at a final level of improvement and that improvement itself becomes the norm rather than the exception. Those who fail to engage in continuous improvement inevitably fall back into the mire of old habits that are no longer as effective as they once were, and they take themselves down the tube. Continuous improvement requires that you seek and embrace failure at increasing levels of scope and frequency.

What You Can Do

The first step in waking up to your competitive agenda-based selling approach is to stop denying that you have one. You do. Own it. Next, pay attention. When you notice yourself working to convince clients, recognize that you are not on a pathway to partnership, even if the transaction goes in your favor. If you find yourself having to strong-arm clients to do what you need them to do in order to get a check for yourself, then you are not fostering partnership, you are engaging in Conspiratorial or Competitive Selling. If you become aware of having to convince clients to comply with your solution and are struggling to prove why your answer is the best way to solve their problem, you are engaged in Consultative Selling. All this robs clients of their power to choose, causing them to resent you. You will regret violating what could have been a worthwhile, long-term client relationship.

The next step is to take your attention off what you will get and shift it toward a commitment-based selling approach and what you will give. The surprise is that selling gets a lot easier when agents, as advisors, and clients are working together rather than against each other. Make a conscious choice that the client's project is of utmost importance and make your project be that their project is fulfilled. Declare this to the client. Make this commitment. Then take actions that are consistent with your declaration. Gone is any need to force clients into making a decision. At every decision point, align your words and actions to the client winning at their game. When you notice that you have reverted to your personal agenda, own that as well. If necessary, tell on yourself, letting the client know that you had gone off course and right the rudder. Likely, they already noticed the difference. Look for yourself. You know when someone is out for number one, don't you?

Be aware that when clients see that you are operating from your own agenda, they will also come from that place, easily drawing you into controlling, manipulating, and ultimately dominating selling conversations. This is them using the tactics, tricks, and techniques that they learned from their teachers or other agents. This takes everyone down the tubes. Your task becomes talking first yourself and then the client back up the tube. Practicing Advisory Selling allows your natural advisory skills to take over, giving you power to build an authentic partnership with your client, and ensuring that a client is fully empowered to choose for themselves. Such skills are already something you possess and simply need to develop. The most exciting thing about the Advisory Selling Method is that it does not teach anything you don't already know. You just don't know that you know it.

PART III
WHAT IS POSSIBLE & EMBRACING THE FUTURE OF SELLING

SELLING AS IT WAS ALWAYS MEANT TO BE

It is only by owning that we as humans can't avoid being deceptive that we can free ourselves to be more inceptive and therefore contribute to others more fully.

CHAPTER SEVEN
ADVISORY SELLING PRINCIPLES
Serving the Client's Best Interest

Advisory Selling differs significantly from the common agenda-based modes of selling. To recap, Conspiratorial Selling, which can be outright criminal, completely ignores the client's best interest and often does damage to the client. Competitive Selling may cause less damage, but it is still adversarial. It is always in the background waiting to undermine an agent-client relationship. Competitive Selling is where agents and clients vie to take advantage of each other, regardless of the cost to the other, and where the selling agent ignores the best interest of the client in an effort to get paid. Consultative Selling is currently the most commonly used because it's client-centric and requires greater trust. When the agent, as a consultant, and client differ on solutions, this trust can break down, resulting in disappointment and defeat. In Consultative Selling, the client comes first, but it's the consultant's job to sell a solution, whether a problem exists for the client or not. In that regard, the solution comes before the client.

When a consultative selling agent inadvertently stumbles upon their natural advisory selling skills, they develop a more collaborative selling relationship and become a highly valued member of the client's team. However, collaboration breaks down when an agenda-based approach gets in the way. If we are able to remain true to a collaborative service-driven selling approach then those same natural advisory skills that were accessed accidently become available for you to access on purpose. This is what the Advisory Selling Method teaches you.

Shifting How You Sell

There are two sides to the selling spectrum. There is the deceptive side and the inceptive side. The deceptive side is agenda-based selling, while the inceptive side is commitment-based selling. It is human nature to be deceptive in selling and we have no choice but to live with that. We can, however, choose to connect with our human spirit and access our natural inceptive selling skills.

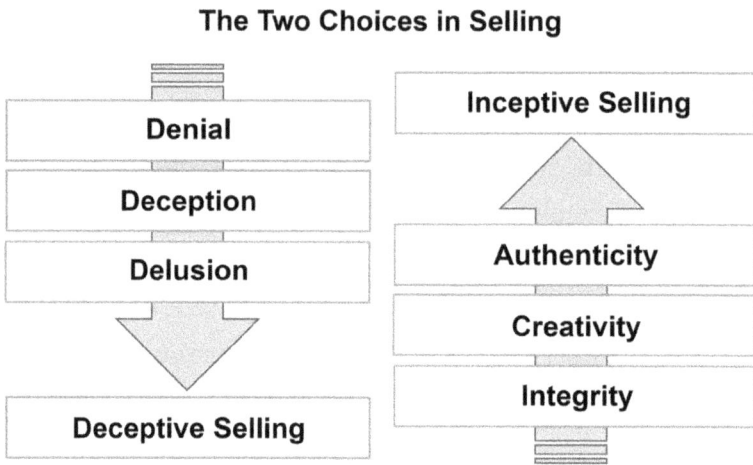

The Two Choices in Selling

Denial
Deception
Delusion

Deceptive Selling

Inceptive Selling

Authenticity
Creativity
Integrity

Many selling agents claim to be an advisor, but that tends to be in name only. Their methods are likely to still be conspiratorial, competitive, or in the best case, consultative. In the 1990s, all sorts of agents positioned themselves as advisors when all they really did was sell their solutions solely for a check while pretending to prioritize client service. Until Consultative Selling came along, selling agent conversations were dominated by conspiratorial or competitive methods. On occasion, a selling agent might advise a client, but only if the outcome served the agent's best interest. Even when a transaction failed to achieve the objectives of the client, the agent still received the commission, and the client paid the price. These agents were selling lies, luring clients in with false promises.

Becoming a Trusted Advisor

Let's compare a pharmaceutical salesperson and a doctor. The pharmaceutical salesperson has a solution looking for a problem. They have a pill to sell. A trusted advisor, like the doctor, formulates a client profile (examination), creates a strategic analysis (diagnosis), and makes a recommendation (prescription). As an advisor, the doctor empowers the patient to make an appropriate choice (treatment), one that produces an intended result (cure) that serves the patient's best interest. The pharmaceutical rep doesn't take this approach. This type of selling agent wants to convince the customer that the pill is the solution. They will work hard to do so because the agent's aim is to sell the pill whether it is needed or not. Since this type of agent isn't concerned about ongoing relationships, they rarely develop repeat business or referrals and are forced to perpetually search for new customers.

Becoming a
Trusted Advisor

Intended Result

↑

Appropriate Choice
Recommendation
Strategic Analysis
Client Profile

Doctors know how to build partnerships with patients. Good doctors put their patients first. They show patients the available options and empower them to make appropriate choices. The difference between a great physician and a pharmaceutical salesman is in their language. A pharmaceutical salesperson talks like an agent. A doctor speaks like a trusted advisor. When we learn the language of an advisor, we can use that as our foundation for building a high level of client trust, and in time, enduring collaborative relationships.

It has been shown in many ways that when working in collaboration, people accomplish so much more than when they are in competition with one another. Our innate ability to work with each other, rather than against each other is what made us the dominant species on the planet. Yet, in spite of our natural ability to collaborate, all we see on the news are people fighting and opposing each other's ideas and innovations. We see little of our species' inherent collaboration skills practiced in the world leaving us to question our ability as humans to work together. There is an answer and that is the Advisory Selling Method.

Advisory Selling shows us how to access this deep well of human spirit by focusing on developing the natural advisory selling skills we all have within us. As previously mentioned, the Reverend Martin Luther King sold people of all races on the concept of saving America's soul by eliminating the apartheid practices embedded in the foundation of our society. His method was the essence of Inceptive Selling. He sold a future that called upon human spirit and fostered a vision that still resonates with us today.

Another religious leader traveled a different and more deceptive path by taking advantage of human nature. He worked to drain the pockets of believers by convincing them that they lacked the power within themselves to deal with their own challenges. His product was a simple 15-cent scrap of linen. For this he required a pledge of $1,000. A woman I once knew put all her faith in this piece of fabric that she was promised would heal her. Rather than going to the doctor, she made the pledge and worked to save the money for that bit of cloth. Sadly, she died of a very curable form of cancer before it arrived. This religious leader's method was the essence of Deceptive Selling.

When the son was cleaning out his mother's home, the phone rang. A woman was looking for the mother and was told she had died. The woman showed no empathy and continued to ask about the most recent $1,000 pledge the mother had made. The son repeated that his mother had passed. She pressed him further, asking who was going to pay the pledge. He again said that she *had died*. The woman promptly hung up showing no interest or empathy. This was human nature based Deceptive Selling disguising itself as an emissary of human spirit. Such a betrayal is a reflection of the competition, conspiracy, conflict, and corruption that limit our world by infecting even our most sacred ideals. This level of betrayal puts our entire world at risk of spiraling into a deeper state of corruption and criminality.

Becoming More Consequential

Advisory Selling is an evolutionary advance shaped by the commitments of human spirit. It involves creativity, collaboration, compassion, and contribution, and puts the client's best interest first. It is shocking how many selling agents claim that they are already doing this. In truth, they are doing the opposite and have no clue that their asserted intent is not being fulfilled. Although they may truly mean well, if you listen closely, their language betrays them. When an agent becomes a trusted advisor by using the Advisory Selling Method, their clients naturally know who they can count on, like the trusted doctor who will always deliver appropriate results.

Human nature, with its relentless potential for deception, is easily dealt with by employing Advisory Selling to effectively address the deceptive behavior of clients. Advisory Selling empowers human spirit because it is based on a commitment to benefit the client. Like a surgeon's scalpel, Advisory Selling cuts through client denial and deception, and the delusion that limits a client's ability to see a way forward.

It offers, through diligent practice, access to the profound creativity we all have, compassion for others that we long to express, collaboration that gets so much more accomplished, and the ability to make a serious contribution to others. This is what being consequential is all about. We all long to be more consequential but the forces of the survival-driven human nature within us can lead us to become criminal. The Advisory Selling Method gives you the language skills needed to shape a more consequential reality for yourself and everyone you touch.

Human Nature + Human Spirit = Human Being

Survival is non-negotiable. We cannot choose between human nature and human spirit because they are permanently bonded like two sides of a coin. But we can choose whether to be deceptive or inceptive when we sell. Since we are all selling all the time, we must make this choice of which side to focus upon.

The Advisory Selling Method teaches inceptive selling that is grounded in our human spirit which requires that we plant a seed of an idea that will serve the recipient's best interest so that they, and everyone around them, are uplifted and empowered. You are already having advisory conversations whether you are aware of it or not and, when you do, you are making the choice to be inceptive. With rigorous practice, the power of our innate inceptive skills can outweigh our deceptive habits. The Advisory Selling Method provides the most viable way of making such a shift.

The Principles of Advisory Selling

The Advisory Selling Method is based on five principles that will squeeze every ounce of deception out of your conversations and ensure that you stay true to your commitment to working in partnership with your clients. This inevitably leads to a significantly greater income in a shorter period of time.

Advisory Selling Principles

- Unstoppable Intention
- Fearless Communication
- Complete Openness
- Genuine Interest
- Authentic Commitment

These principles eliminate any chance of falling into deceptive selling and open the door to inceptive selling. On this inceptive side of selling, there are five principles that are the underpinnings upon which Advisory Selling is built. The first principle is the demonstration of an *authentic commitment* to serving the best interest of clients. The second is *genuine interest* in the client's situation and needs, and third is *complete openness* to whatever outcome will best assist the client in accomplishing their project. The fourth principle of Advisory Selling is *fearless communication* in the face of risking the client relationship by telling them what they do not want to hear when they need to hear it. Ultimately, there must be *unstoppable intention* to serve the best interest of the client at all costs, which is the fifth core principle.

An agent, as a trusted advisor, must commit to each of these principles in order for clients to win. As advisors, they have got to take their attention off themselves and put it fully on the client. The great surprise is that the more the focus is on helping the client get what they want, the more the agent will also get what they want. In Advisory Selling when the client wins, the advisor wins.

Authentic Commitment

By being authentically committed to serving the client's best interest, you establish a foundation of trust as an advisor and garner tenacious loyalty from a client. Clients naturally gravitate to those they know will do everything needed to ensure that their best interest is served. "Authentic" means to be really committed; it is not pretense. Commitment does not equate with a wish, hope, or dream. It means absolute resolve to accomplish a desired outcome that will benefit the client. Clients have come to expect an inauthentic commitment that is conveyed with a great deal of posturing, pretending, and proving, none of which is truly authentic. There is nothing you can do to prove that you are authentically committed. You simply must *be* authentically committed and your actions will follow in accord with complete openness, honesty, integrity, and consistency of purpose.

Genuine Interest

The biggest generator of interest from clients is being interested in them. Being genuinely captivated by the client's situation, their needs, and their desires for the future is what makes the advisor equally interesting to the client. Pretending to be interested only lasts so long. The attention of clients tends to wane when selling agents are trying too hard to impress them or push them. Clients are most interested in themselves and often could care less about an agent or advisor. They care about themselves and what they want to accomplish. They will only be interested in you if you are offering to help them accomplish what they want. The value lies in the difference between getting attention from the audience and giving it to them. Advisory Selling is the same way. It helps you learn to take your attention off of yourself and put it on the client. The performer who captures the interest of their audience is not the one who emphasizes how they look; it's about how they connect.

It isn't always easy to be truly interested in others, but it is paramount to building a productive partnership. People automatically evaluate, judge, and condemn other people before they even meet them. This pre-judgment of others is a blindfold that makes connecting with clients more difficult, if not impossible. Because clients are rarely as we perceive them to be, the surprise about the reality of who they are sparks the delight we feel once we place our attention on what matters most to them. The agent, as an advisor, must generate a real regard for what matters most to clients. It is at this moment that advisors immediately become of greater interest to the client.

When a selling agent fails to show interest in clients, this undermines an advisory relationship and invites the client to treat the agent as nothing more than a disposable convenience. It is the difference between thinking you already have all the answers for the client and being willing to ask the questions that will bring out the essence of the client. Therefore, being a person who is naturally interested in others unleashes the power of human connection.

Complete Openness

Making the client's project your number one priority is what's required to operate with complete openness. Being willing to let go of your own agenda and fully embrace the client's project is the primary task of this third principle of Advisory Selling. Being completely open to whatever outcome will best serve the client, even one that means no income to the advisor, is not a typical practice demonstrated in selling situations. Usually, the agent is driven by multiple agendas. At minimum, these are one for his company and one for himself, and they both are about making money. For the company that may be about meeting expenses or making the stockholders happy. For the agent, it is most often about making money to pay rent, putting food on the table, making the boss look good, and keeping their job; it's about survival.

When you are in survival mode and only selling to meet your basic needs, the ability to remain detached is difficult to access and our ability to serve a client's best interest shuts down. In these circumstances, it takes real courage to detach, let go of your fear, and focus on the client's best outcome. Attachment is even harder to break when you are riding high on the expectations of future compensation. If you are working with a bigger client than usual, you can easily get attached to the idea of a bigger pay out than usual and blow the opportunity.

Sometimes companies promote fierce competitiveness within their organization, a competitiveness that makes it even more difficult for agents to let go of concerns about their own survival and focus on being of service to the client and the client completing their project. The cultivation of competition as part of the selling culture is automatic and mechanical. Ironically, the competition is meant to make the selling agents and the firm more successful. Instead, companies must grind through many clients who spread feedback which negatively impacts agent success, company viability, and brand.

One may ask, "If I'm successful even when my agenda takes precedence over that of the client's project, why not continue with that approach?" There are several reasons. First is that you must bury your sense of spirit, which makes for a compromised existence in the midst of available abundance. Second, that kind of success is achieved by very few and is not sustainable. Third, success at the expense of others always peaks, and you will eventually find yourself crashing to the bottom. You may be following the laws of human nature, but you are violating the laws of human spirit which always find a way to teach us hard lessons. Detachment is a high-risk choice that may feel scary, but it is the only doorway to building real client relationships.

Detachment is power. As it turns out, the more you are detached from your agenda and a particular outcome, the easier it is to generate business and take it to successful completion. The agent's detachment removes the competition between agent and client over who is going to win, freeing the client, and empowering them to make appropriate choices when presented with challenges.

Not only is detachment a source of real power, it is the source of true advisor-client collaboration and partnership. No longer do you have to worry about the client taking all the credit when the deal works out or blaming you if it does not. Remaining detached from a particular outcome and showing up only in support of the client achieving their project moves you into the position of trusted advisor.

Fearless Communication

In Advisory Selling, it is necessary to demonstrate a willingness to tell clients what they need to hear even when they don't want to hear it, and even if it risks the relationship. If you are unwilling to risk a relationship with a client, you will never have one. Collaborative partnerships with clients are more easily built when the trusted advisor has the courage to say what the client needs to hear, saving both the client and the advisor from going down the tube. Advisor leadership is the only thing that can pull a client out of their tailspin of denial, deception, and delusion. Clients who deny the facts are destined to deceive others about those facts and get trapped believing their own lies as the truth. This can result in devastating consequences for clients and, even more so, for the selling agents who fail to be advisors. Clients inevitably come back to berate the selling agent for their own mistake, asking why the agent did not tell them what might happen. If the agent failed to tell the client for fear of offending the client, they deserve to be held responsible. When clients are fearlessly informed, they come back and ask for help, acknowledging that they should have listened. These are the clients with whom an advisor can build stronger, more enduring, and effective collaborative partnerships.

In Advisory Selling, trusted advisors develop their capacity for leadership. This means they work to see things that clients have failed to consider. It also means that they make greater demands on themselves than they would ever make of anyone else. Because of this, they have the power to demand of clients things that a client would never demand of themselves. They give clients powerful choices and bring forth leadership from within the client so that, together, they can achieve the client's desired outcome.

More often than not, selling agents attempt to control the client. This is the opposite of leadership. Leadership means giving up control in order to take command. Leaders must be willing to say things no one else will dare to say, especially when few want to hear the truth. They are not afraid to upset people, especially when those people need their applecart to be overturned. If the best interest of the client is to be served, the Advisory Selling advisor cannot afford to allow the client to take control of the process. The advisor, by stepping in, prevents the client from getting in their own way, even becoming their own worst enemy, robbing themselves of a successful outcome.

Unstoppable Intention

Unstoppable intention can be defined as a total commitment to operating in such a way that the client's best interest is served regardless of the consequences. Like authentic commitment, intentionality is a quality of being that does not involve doing. It may generate action but is not, in and of itself, an action. The power of intention comes from within. It only flows in one direction, it is future focused, and any conscious action taken is born of that intention. If you've ever intended to arrive at a destination on time and left late, yet still arrived with time to spare, you've experienced the power of intention.

When we direct our attention toward the fulfillment of the client's vision, we pave the way for the client and circumstances to align along that same pathway. Since intention only flows in one direction, there is only one way that it can go, the way we intend. Unstoppable intention results in something happening regardless of the challenges, complications, or circumstances that attempt to get in the way.

All too often we expect things to go a certain way. And many times, they don't because we fail to exercise our innate power of intention. By not defining a clear intention, we default to expectation, which produces nothing. People often confuse expectation and intention. They are quite the opposite. Expectation is simply the belief that others or circumstances should somehow give us what we want. When our expectations are not fulfilled, we get upset. Placing our attention on our intention through inspection is essential in selling. When you take the time to inspect and question whether your expectations are achievable, you are operating with intention. Anything you put your attention on through inspection, whether that be a relationship, more money, or a new job, will succeed. When you fail to inspect, you can only expect, not intend, which is a recipe for things not turning out the way you want.

Emotions can be another obstacle to producing the results you want. Emotions, scientifically, are simply peptides flowing through the bloodstream. The greater the emotion, the more intense the drama, which is the BS that traps us in our subjective reality where access to creativity is denied. Emotions are often a killer of intention. Intention can only operate in the objective reality of facts that opens the door to the truth that is not available in the subjective world of lies. Much like drugs, we easily become addicted to the peptide cocktail of emotions which limits our ability to take action where needed, inhibiting our performance. Emotion is not relevant when it comes to performance. It's your intention. Your intention leads to action that allows you to perform at an elevated level in service to your clients; it requires that you put aside emotions to best assist clients in producing their desired results.

An example of this is two people in the same foxhole under brutal attack. They have a choice to make. One leaps out of the foxhole and takes action that changes the course of the battle. The other remains in the foxhole. The difference is not in the emotions of the men, they both have the same fears and circumstances, but they make different choices. One person chooses to fulfill his intention, and one person gets lost in his emotions, which causes him to be paralyzed by fear. Therefore, one is branded the hero, and one is branded the coward.

When a client is on the fence with a transaction, the sheer focus of the subtle energy of your intention will push the deal over to the appropriate side. Intention may be accompanied with fear, but it should not be clouded by doubt. Fear can be a powerful driver as many champions and great performers have attested. Doubt cannot be a factor. If you need to doubt something, doubt your doubts.

Intention aligns with "I can! I shall! I will! I must!" There is no wishing, hoping, or longing. Intention comes from the idea that a result has already been accomplished, that the game has already been won. Intention does not ask us to consider if something will happen, it focuses on when. In Advisory Selling, serving the best interest of clients, at all costs and against all odds, even against client self-sabotage, is the only acceptable outcome.

What You Can Do

Practice, practice, practice. Practice noticing when you are not bringing the Advisory Selling Principles into a conversation. The Advisory Selling Principles are the root cause of every successful selling event.

You may think that the various techniques you've been using are responsible for the success you have experienced thus far. Nothing could be further from the truth. It has been your advisory skills all along. Your innate advisory skills are, in fact, producing the results you are having. But these skills are limited because they are buried underneath all the layers of the common selling habits you've developed.

You must choose who you want to be. Will you choose to be a conspirator? a competitor? a consultant? a collaborator? or an advisor? Your choice defines both the quality of your life and the impact you have on others. If you choose to deceive your customers, you must then settle for an ugly grind in which you will soon run out of victims. This is a one-way ticket down a self-destructive tube. If, however, you are looking to escape the bondage of your survival-driven human nature you must learn the Advisory Selling Method to become true to yourself and bring out your natural service-driven advisory skills. Acting with Authentic Commitment, Genuine Interest, Complete Openness, Fearless Communication, and Unstoppable Intention will lead to the life of contribution, recognition, reward, and fulfillment that comes with that way of being human.

The principles, practices, and processes of Advisory Selling apply in all areas of life. Parents can sell their children on ideas that will prepare them for the future. Teachers can sell their students on ways to study harder and become more knowledgeable. Managers can sell their team members on methods aimed at elevating their performance, reward, and recognition. Consultants can sell their clients on ways to maximize client benefits. Coaches can sell their players on methods that will ensure their success. This is because coaches have the unique ability to bring out from within the brilliance of another person.

Advisory Selling skills are available to everyone who chooses to develop them with the Advisory Selling Method. As previously stated, accomplishing this will take diligence and devoted practice, but you will find a new level of freedom in this way of selling that will make it all worth it. To be cliché, you will get out of it what you put into it. Selling will prove increasingly easy, efficient, effective, empowering, and enjoyable, the more you practice. As you know, the more you enjoy doing something, the better you will be at it. Your compensation will be greater recognition and reward, bringing you increased satisfaction and fulfillment.

Since new opportunities rarely just fall in our laps, learning the skills of deal generation help us overcome our fear of the unknown and risk starting something new.

Chapter Eight
Generating Opportunities
The First Three Modules of the Advisory Selling Method

If a productive selling relationship is in the cards, the Advisory Selling Method is the most effective and most high-velocity way to get there. Advisory Selling puts the client's best interest ahead of all other priorities. Your engagement with the ASM will change how you listen to others, how you speak to them, how you think about them, and who you become to them. Being a trusted advisor by using the Advisory Selling Method is different than being a consultant. The consultant's job is to come up with answers to a problem. The advisor's job is to ask the questions that empower a client to come up with their own solutions in accord with what the client truly wants.

The truth is that you already have within you everything you need. We all have these skills, but since we lack a clear method for bringing them out, developing them, and putting them to work, they stay dormant until some major life event draws them to the surface. Certain events are important enough that they are triggered to arise from within us. And, because in retrospect, we see that we have already used them, we know that we do have them within us. The challenge is learning to discern these natural skills from the many layers of techniques and tricks we've learned to use to influence the actions of others. Our natural skills are available all the time, but until we learn to intentionally access and apply them, we cannot use them to make a difference.

It takes courage to give up your familiar habits and what may have worked in the past to take on a new way of doing things that seems counterintuitive to everything you've learned so far. The options available to you are clear. Whether it is working or not, you could keep doing what you have been doing and learn to live with the same outcomes you have experienced thus far. You might try looking outside of yourself for a new set of techniques hoping they will give you the results you want and need, which they won't. Or, you can learn the Advisory Selling Method, and take the risk of finding the answers you need within yourself and change everything for the better.

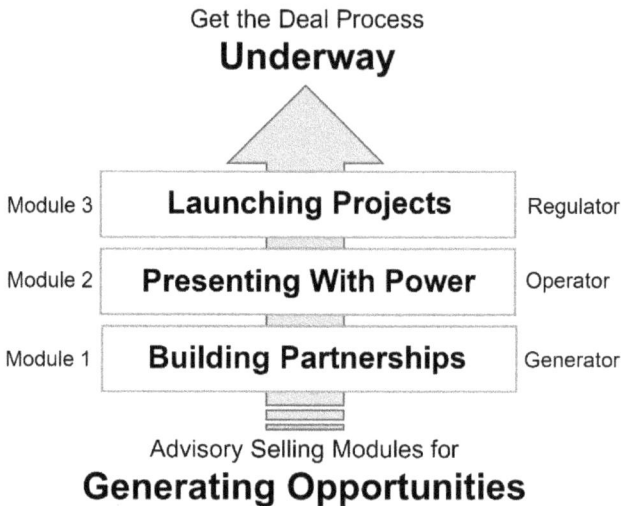

Get the Deal Process
Underway

Module 3	**Launching Projects**	Regulator
Module 2	**Presenting With Power**	Operator
Module 1	**Building Partnerships**	Generator

Advisory Selling Modules for
Generating Opportunities

In Advisory Selling, there are six modules that teach specific language skills which convert your conversation with clients from an agenda-based selling conversation into a commitment-based advisory one. The first three of the six are modules for generating opportunities. Agents, as trusted advisors, need to focus both on developing their deal generation skills and on how important it is to master connecting with clients. When looking at generating income, it is important to ask yourself if you are focused on selling the product or helping the person accomplish their project. While it is essential to have a good product and complete product knowledge, that isn't enough to access the power to influence others to take an appropriate action. People write checks; products do not.

There is no deal execution without deal generation. If you're going to get paid and increase your income, you have to first develop your ability to generate business. To develop your deal generation language skills so that they become your dominant mode of influence, you need to learn the skill development methods presented in these three ASM Generating Opportunities modules. This means that, in addition to being strong on the transactional side by knowing your product and process, you need to get stronger on the people side of the equation.

Module 1: Building Partnerships

The first learning module of the Advisory Selling Method is called Building Partnerships, which is exactly what it does. Partnership is the product of the advisor and the client getting clear on the client's project, the advisor offering to help them accomplish that project, and the client accepting the advisor's offer to assist the client in getting from where they currently are to where they want to be in the future. Without a project, there is no partnership.

In the Building Partnership learning module, you learn three practices for working collaboratively with clients. The first is Evoking Rapport, the second is Generating Projects, and the third is Forging Partnership.

	Practice 1	**Evoking Rapport**	Generator
Module 1 **Building Partnerships**	Practice 2	**Generating Projects**	Operator
	Practice 3	**Forging Partnership**	Regulator

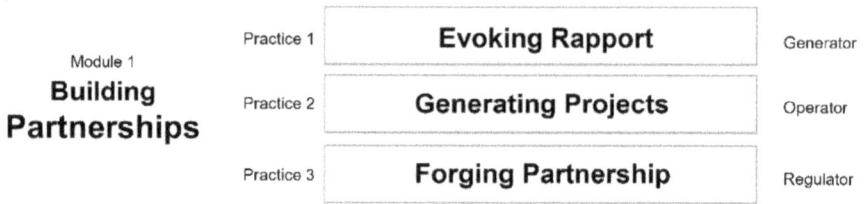

In normal selling conversations, there is little opportunity to practice these essential skills needed to build partnerships. With these three practices, the deal process goes much smoother, there is more certainty of deal completion, and a more enduring advisor-client relationship is likely. All of which equates to more income.

Practice 1: Evoking Rapport

Evoking Rapport is the first step to building partnership. This practice shifts the Advisory Selling conversation away from what is normally a competition to see who knows best toward a natural collaboration in which client and trusted advisor work together to explore an opportunity. While this practice is listed here, the truth is that it is important to evoke rapport at the beginning of every conversation.

People have a lot of ideas about rapport, most of which have nothing to do with rapport. Commenting on the stuffed blue marlin hanging on a wall or a family photo can make for a nice chat, but that has nothing to do with rapport. There is no depth or commitment in it. What rapport makes available is a basis for a meaningful relationship where trust is present.

	Step 1	**Opening**	Lead
	Step 2	**Permission**	Ground
Practice 1	Step 3	**Interest**	Key
Evoking	Step 4	**Detachment**	Offer
Rapport	Step 5	**Questions**	Transition

Rapport is present when you successfully open up the client's automatic protective listening so that they become more receptive. That happens when you identify the primary concern of the client. Only then will they be open to your offer to work with them to accomplish a project that is important to them.

After opening the client's receptive listening, you next need to ask their permission, in one way or another, to get into their private world and bring ideas that could change their world. This is difficult for some clients who are not practiced at being open and vulnerable, especially not with "salespeople." Once you have asked for permission, you don't have to wait for their answer. If they don't explicitly say no then they are saying yes in their head. You next need to demonstrate that you are more interested in them and their project then trying to be interesting to them. What will make you interesting to them is your interest in them.

Next, you need to communicate to the client that their agenda is your agenda, that you have no agenda of your own other than for them to accomplish their project and get to where they want to be. The way to do that is to ask them questions about their situation and how they go to where they are currently. When they give short answers like "Great!" or "Pretty tough," ask why-based questions to elicit more of their story so you have more to work with.

Practice 2: Generating Projects

Before we look at how to generate projects, let's reestablish what I mean by "project." A project, for our purposes, has three components: where the client is currently, where they want to get to in the future, and how you, as a trusted advisor, can help get them there.

The Evoking Rapport practice converts normal client protective listening into greater receptive listening. Only when this happens can you begin to explore the client's project. To get clear about a client's project, start by asking about the client's accomplishments. This opens a doorway to the client telling the history of their situation. The degree to which the client is telling you their story is the degree of rapport you have with them.

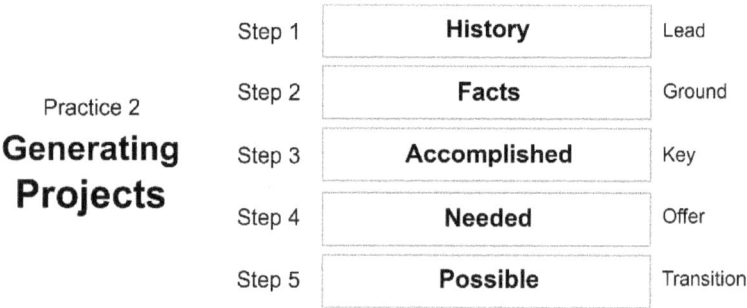

Practice 2 **Generating Projects**	Step 1	**History**	Lead
	Step 2	**Facts**	Ground
	Step 3	**Accomplished**	Key
	Step 4	**Needed**	Offer
	Step 5	**Possible**	Transition

You want to learn about their history, what has brought them to where they are right now. We can call this "history" because, as the client tells their story, they are telling you less about the objective facts of what happened and more about their interpretation of what happened. When clients assign meaning to the fact of their personal experience they are operating from their subjective reality. They believe that their tale is the truth. It is not. This is their Big Story or "BS," as I like to call it.

Like with evoking rapport, if you were to ask a client a question and they give a quick response, you should ask some "why-based" questions so their story will come pouring out and so that you get a sufficient amount of story out onto the table. As the client speaks, listen. Then, ask fact-based questions to cut through the veneer of the story and get to the truth. These fact-based questions need to be based on what the client has said, not some random, probing questions from off the top of your head. Asking questions about what the client said is talking with clients, not at them.

Articulate to the client what you see they have accomplished. This will be evident from the answers that they gave to your fact-based questions. No matter the facts of the situation and how negative they may be, there is always something that can be declared as an accomplishment. Sometimes, it might be that they simply made it through and are still standing. Next, elicit from the client what they see is needed that can be put in place to get them to where they want to be in the future with your help. Use the truths uncovered by your fact-based questions to create, with the client, a vision of a future possibility that is compelling enough to change the client's actions in the present. This is the working definition of selling within the Advisory Selling Method.

Practice 3: Forging Partnership

Now that the client's project is clear, a partnership can be forged. Partnership is what gets created when the advisor and the client align on working together to accomplish the client's project. We forge partnership all the time, but we may be unaware that we are doing it, and therefore, do it poorly. As a trusted advisor, you intentionally declare the partnership into existence, formalizing the agreement so that the advisor's resources can be set in motion on the client's behalf.

	Step 1	**Risks**	Lead
Practice 3	Step 2	**Responsibility**	Ground
Forging Partnership	Step 3	**Declaration**	Key
	Step 4	**Invitation**	Offer
	Step 5	**Promise**	Transition

In partnership, both risks and responsibility must be dealt with to lay the foundation for a productive relationship. The trusted advisor leads the way by initiating frank conversations that get the risks out on the table rather than avoiding, covering up, or diminishing them. There needs to be no question, for the client, about the potential impact of these risks and the need for partnership with you as an advisor to help face them. After openly identifying the risks and their potential impact, the next conversation to have is about what the client needs to be responsible for. Laying this out at this point works to remove any uncertainty about their project being completed successfully. It must be clear to the client what they themselves are responsible to contribute to the partnership to maximize the value of working with you, their trusted advisor.

Now that these conversations have been had, you can declare the partnership into existence. Inside of that declaration, declare the client's capability to execute a project successfully and declare your commitment to the client's success in order for the client to remove the self-doubt at the core of any inaction on their part. The next step is to issue to the client a clear invitation that offers the opportunity to work together, makes a promise, and locks in partnership. This is a verbal contract of some form that defines the manner in which you will work together and outlines what benefits will accrue to both the client and you, the trusted advisor. This promise is for the outcomes that will be produced as a result of the client accepting the invitation to go forward, in partnership with you, with certainty that their quest to achieve the future they have envisioned, will be achieved.

With partnership, any deal process will go much smoother. This means that an agent, as an advisor, can conduct more deals at the same time. Partnership makes long-term client-advisor relationships possible, bringing with it the capacity to make more money in the future.

Module 2: Presenting with Power

The second learning module is called Presenting with Power. This module focuses on an approach to presentations that allows the audience to receive, retain, and replicate your message. To deliver a truly powerful presentation, you must tell the audience the purpose of the presentation and why it is important to them. Then follow the old broadcast rule "Tell them what you are going to tell them, tell them, and then tell them what you have told them."

To do this, you build a presentation based on a set of principles that ensures your message has both the power to move people to act and the clarity needed for them to get others on board, even in the face of resistance. This is especially important when they must deal with partners, financial advisors, and family members who will call their recount of the presentation into question. Your offer must be delivered in a way that the client can talk about that offer in the same manner as you. When you're talking, that's called marketing. When they're talking with others, that's called branding. Essentially, the clients become part of your sales force.

Module 2 **Presenting with Power**	Practice 1	**Strategic Analysis**	Generator
	Practice 2	**Positioning Value**	Operator
	Practice 3	**Building Presentations**	Regulator

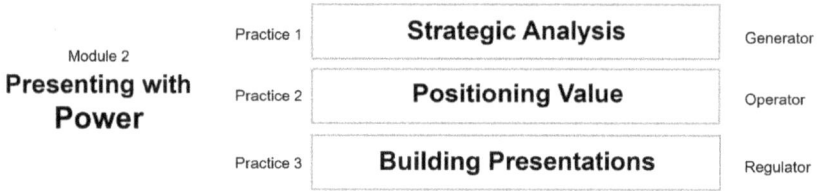

To package a presentation with power, you need to fully understand a client's current situation, where they want to take things in the future, and the options available to them. This is achieved through a strategic analysis. Positioning the value that your platform, people, and process provide as something that will help the client resolve their current problems and accomplish their project naturally follows. Finally, the presentation must be built.

In this module, it is important to understand that Practice 3 – Building Presentations entails always following the same steps in the same order to maximize the power of your message. Unlike the practices that you practice the same way over and over, so that you can ultimately innovate, this process is fixed, where the steps are followed to the letter and in proper order.

Practice 1: Strategic Analysis

Building a Strategic Analysis of the client's current circumstances helps them to better understand their situation and the options available to them so they can make an appropriate choice. Before beginning this analysis, make sure you are aligned with the client's project of getting from where they are to where they want to be. Investors, businesses, and individuals have different types of projects. Work with the client to clarify your understanding of where they stand currently with their endeavors and where they want to be in the future.

	Step 1	**Project**	Lead
	Step 2	**Factors**	Ground
Practice 1	Step 3	**Options**	Key
Strategic Analysis	Step 4	**Strategy**	Offer
	Step 5	**Recommendation**	Transition

From there, draw out with questions the client's current challenges that affect their situation and that could get in the way of them accomplishing their project. These factors may be with their asset, business, people, financials, or legal or market situations and they may have implications that affect the project. Identifying these factors brings present the challenges that might have significant future implications. Once the challenges have been identified, lay out a minimum of three options of actions that the client might take to fulfill their project along with the consequences and the accompanying risks for each.

The next step is to have a conversation with the client about their strategic objectives. This could include immediate actions for them to take, their short-term objectives and long-term vision, what their exit strategy is and/or what their legacy plan might be for their beneficiaries. Having laid this foundation, the job of an agent, as an advisor, is to then give the client a clear choice between all of the available options and to make a recommendation of the best option that helps the client avert imminent challenges and accomplish their project. Having laid all the cards on the table, the client is empowered to choose. This practice, like all of the Advisory Selling practices, is inceptive, eductive, and service-driven. It encompasses the five core principles of the ASM: authentic commitment, genuine interest, complete openness, fearless communication, and unstoppable intention.

Practice 2: Positioning Value

With this second practice you position your value demonstrating that you are able to help the client deal with potentially undermining factors and pursue the option that will best serve them. Many selling agents make the mistake of promoting their capabilities before they ever find out what the client needs. In Advisory Selling you must flip the script, and only promote your capabilities after you fully understand the needs of a client and their project. This will help the client see why they should choose you. Having completed the strategic analysis, it is now time to talk about what you bring to the table.

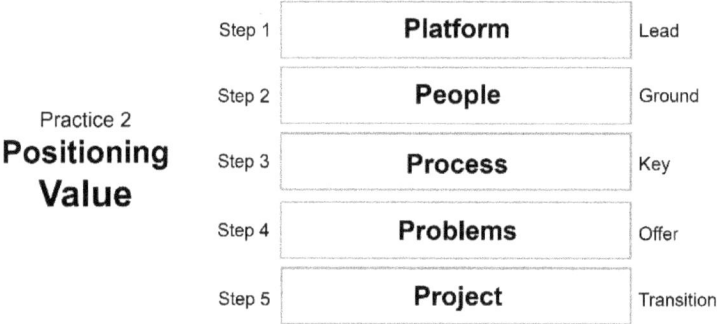

	Step		
	Step 1	**Platform**	Lead
Practice 2	Step 2	**People**	Ground
Positioning Value	Step 3	**Process**	Key
	Step 4	**Problems**	Offer
	Step 5	**Project**	Transition

To assure the client of your ability to help them achieve what they want, it is essential to disclose how you will deliver your services. Once the challenges are fully understood this practice positions how the challenges will be dealt with in order to ensure a client can get from where they stand today to where they want to be in the future. You do this by giving clients a clear understanding of the platform you will use to deliver the results you have been asked to help the client achieve. This might include company and team capabilities, resources, and a track record of results.

Then paint a clear picture for the client of the specific people who will engage in supporting them in achieving their project. Provide details about any unique capabilities or experience in dealing with issues that the client is facing. Take the time to explain the step-by-step process that the team will undertake on their behalf and how that process leads, with more power, velocity, and certainty, to the results the client is looking to achieve.

The next step is to make clear to the client how this team, following this process, and operating on this platform will turn the challenges they are facing into essential stepping-stones to the fulfillment of the client's project. Present to the client, in detail, the future that will become available to them so that the client can begin, with greater clarity and certainty, the process of preparing to step into that future.

By describing your company platform, people, and process, you show the client how you can help them solve any immediate problems and work with them to accomplish their project. Once you have both the necessary client information and a description of your capabilities, you can now build a powerful presentation that will show a clear pathway for the client to the future they want and your ability to help them achieve that end.

Practice 3: Building Presentations

As mentioned, the third part of this module is a practice that is an entire process for a powerful presentation conversation, or any conversation for that matter. The purpose of the Building Presentations practice is to package your content in such a way that your audience can easily receive, retain, and replicate your message.

	Step 1	**Concept**	Lead
Practice 3	Step 2	**Context**	Ground
Building	Step 3	**Construct**	Key
Presentations	Step 4	**Content**	Offer
	Step 5	**Completion**	Transition

Working downward, the first three phases of this process are Concept, Context, and Construct. Concept means you tell the audience where the presentation is headed, what the purpose is, and how the purpose will be approached. This aligns their listening so that they're able to follow the direction of the presentation to the end. Context means you tell them why this presentation is important to them so that they are more likely to pay attention. Construct means telling them what will be covered in the presentation. This sets the audience up to follow you step-by-step through your presentation so they become better prepared to receive your message. Once these three points have been established, the audience is ready to fully listen to your content and follow you through to completion.

When you fail to package your message in this manner, the audience does not see where they're going, why it's important to them, or how they are going to get there. Many selling agents fail to include the elements of the first three phases in their presentations, typically jumping to page one of their proposal instead. The chances of the audience listening for anything other than what they want to hear is very slim.

The Content is the "meat and potatoes" of your presentation. To be fully effective, you need to move through the concept, context, and construct to structure each section of your presentation. This gives clients the opportunity to take just one bite of juicy "steak" at a time, allowing them to fully digest the meat of your presentation. Inside of this structure, each section of content in your presentation will be, in and of itself, a miniature presentation with all five phases incorporated. This is telling them what you came to tell them in a way that ensures a better chance of them retaining the message. The final part of your presentation is called Completion in which you review the initial three parts of your presentation: Concept, Context, and Construct. From there, use the Forging Partnership Practice from Module 1 to establish a partnership with the client.

Be aware, clients rarely judge us solely on our content, but more so on our delivery so following this process is key to successfully delivering a memorable presentation that will compel clients to take action.

Module 3: Launching Projects

The third learning module is called Launching Projects. It teaches you to define the challenges your clients are facing, to design a complete project that can be achieved, and to install guardrails that will keep that project on track to its final destination. The three practices in this module are the prime ingredients needed to help clients understand how to maximize the value they can derive from working with you.

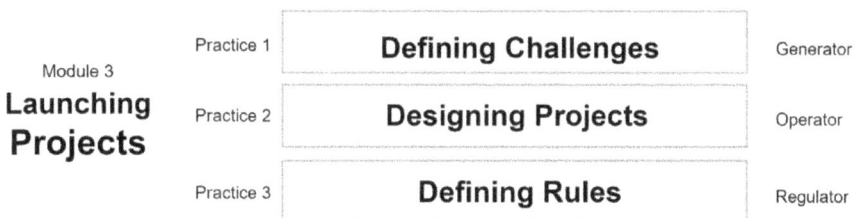

Module 3 Launching Projects	Practice 1	**Defining Challenges**	Generator
	Practice 2	**Designing Projects**	Operator
	Practice 3	**Defining Rules**	Regulator

Usually, both clients and agents assume that they know how a project will roll out based on past experiences. But that is a recipe for disaster. The client is likely to assume that you will work with them in the same way as their previous agent. Agents often assume that the client knows exactly what the agent intends to do, but clients do not. In this scenario, clients end up disappointed when you fail to deliver what they expected based on their previous experiences. When a client's expectations are unfulfilled, they get upset. Expectations almost always lead to making the other person the bad guy. When a deal works out, the client takes the credit, and when it doesn't work out, the agent gets the blame.

Practice 1: Defining Challenges

This is a very challenging practice. It risks penetrating the client's façade of having it all together, when they never do, and makes it possible to bring to the forefront challenges that are initially hidden that could later emerge to thwart the execution of a project.

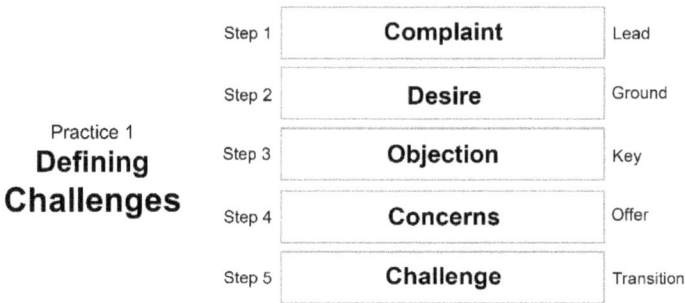

Practice 1 Defining Challenges			
	Step 1	**Complaint**	Lead
	Step 2	**Desire**	Ground
	Step 3	**Objection**	Key
	Step 4	**Concerns**	Offer
	Step 5	**Challenge**	Transition

The first step is to listen closely for client complaints, knowing that they are the gold bars of innovation, the raw material for designing a future worth having. If you are driving down a road in the desert and you see a sign that says "complaints," start digging. You'll find those gold bars. Just look for yourself at a complaint you have regularly and see if you can identify some unmet yearning or aspiration. While agents tend to avoid complaints, they are, in fact, the ticket to success.

You can recognize a complaint when a person says the words, "I don't like…" as in "I don't like where the economy is headed." Where there are complaints, inevitably there are unfulfilled desires. Unearthing that desire is step two. A desire always starts with "I want." Normally when a client is asked to state their desire, what they say is superficial and limited. They might state, "I want to make more money" or "I want to retire." Advisors draw out a client's deeper longings by asking why-based questions and listening for what the client wants that they do not yet have. Asking the key question "Why is that important?" for every client response will bring out the fullness of the client's desire. For example, their bigger desire might be to create a financial foundation for a future family that does not yet exist or a retirement that comes soon enough to enjoy.

The third step in Defining Challenges is getting to the reason why the client has not yet fulfilled their desire. This is called their "objection," which is what they don't want to have to do in order to achieve their desire. The client's objection is usually expressed as "I don't want to have to do…" This stance stops their progress and sets up a contradiction between their desire and their objection. A contradiction is two things that are working in opposition to each other. No surprise, this is where clients, and all people for that matter, get stuck. The purpose of this practice is to get them unstuck.

To do this, you need to have a conversation with the client and explore their concerns. There are two concerns that are sure to arise. The first is about the future if things do not change. This usually paints a picture of more of the same or worse. The second concern is about the future if things did change which may threaten to disrupt what's already working for the client. You will hear these concerns by listening for anything the client says that sounds like "I am afraid...." People become paralyzed by this contradiction in that they are terrified of giving up what they already know, even if the unknown is everything they want. In this way, people organize their lives to avoid what they most want and deserve.

The only way out of this trap is to generate a paradox – that is, two opposites working together rather than against each other in contradiction. Three examples of paradox in action are a blimp, a bicycle, and an airplane. A blimp is heavier than air but uses gas, which is lighter than air; therefore, it can go up and down. Riding a bicycle involves falling and not falling at the same time so we can ride. The Wright Brothers, when inventing the airplane, solved 13 paradoxes to get something in the air and keep it there.

When there is a paradox, a doorway opens to a new set of actions that could not be seen before. The challenge is distinguishing what must change within the client if they are to step through that doorway to a new future in which their objections become the very stepping stones to the fulfillment of their desire. Having the client embrace this paradox empowers them to move toward completion. The challenge needs to be stated as "We must find a way." This positions that paradox in a way that empowers the client and their project, moving the project toward completion. Advisors must apply this practice to compel clients to take action. Defining Challenges, as a practice, is crucial to launching projects and is a vital part of Advisory Selling.

Practice 2: Designing Projects

Once you have defined the client's challenge and opened a doorway in the client's new way of thinking about their situation, you can assist them in designing their project. It is important that you work with them to formulate a pathway for accomplishing their project in real and specific terms. Primary to this objective is installing a practical roadmap that will ensure that, once launched on the right track, the project will stay on track through to its successful completion.

	Step 1	**Mission**	Lead
Practice 2	Step 2	**Objectives**	Ground
Designing	Step 3	**Conditions**	Key
Projects	Step 4	**Metrics**	Offer
	Step 5	**Milestones**	Transition

To start, work with your client to craft a clear mission that is aligned with their project and will benefit the client and the people that they are engaged with. This mission must be a bold view of the future; one that is compelling enough to move them to act. This will help to guide the project design. Next, together with the client create, in specific terms, the objectives that must be attained in order to fulfill this mission. These need to be clear and achievable within a time frame that is consistent with the client's project and will guide the actions of those involved in accomplishing the project. Putting the necessary conditions in place so that these objectives can be effectively taken on is the next step to set the project up for success.

Every project and its mission need some objective means by which to measure project status and momentum. So, having completed the steps above, partner with your client to determine the metrics that will be used to measure performance. The information provided by the metrics will be invaluable in making sure that the project stays on track. Setting milestones is the final step of the Designing Projects practice.

Lay out a plan, once the metrics are clear, that shows how those metrics will be fulfilled over time in specific milestones of accomplishment that mark the progress of the project toward future success. Remember, a project is simply a projection into the future.

Practice 3: Defining Rules

To keep a project on track, the rules of engagement need to be defined. These rules are the requirements for maintaining the partnership and forwarding the project. Determine who the key players are. Find out who the decision makers will be with respect to the project priorities, to include any hidden decision makers or silent partners and all the primary influencers who will shape the decision-making process. This must be clearly defined prior to launching. There can be no hidden decision makers, such as a spouse, other family member, or silent partner, waiting in the wings who will unexpectedly appear and impact the outcome. Besides decision makers, there are influencers that can also significantly affect the deal process because they tend to be cautious or negative when the client turns to them for advice. People such as attorneys, accountants, or investment advisors might be among these influencers. These individuals need to be identified and taken into account.

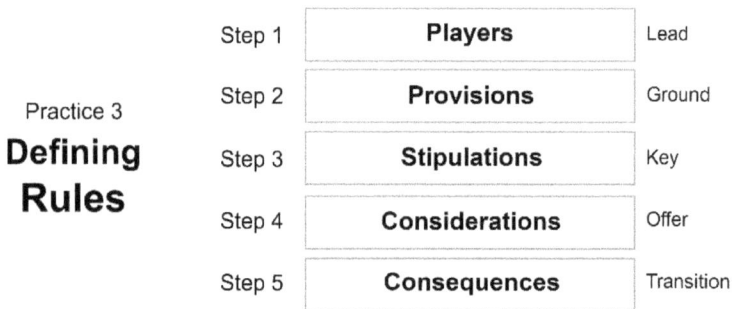

Practice 3 **Defining Rules**	Step 1	**Players**	Lead
	Step 2	**Provisions**	Ground
	Step 3	**Stipulations**	Key
	Step 4	**Considerations**	Offer
	Step 5	**Consequences**	Transition

The next step is to get clear about what each partner will provide for the other and for the deal. These are the provisions. They work to ensure that all parties to the project provide what is needed to move the project forward. This starts to set up a structure of accountability and responsibility. Once the provisions are clear, it is essential to lay out stipulations, the rules of engagement, that define the conduct and communications that will further ensure that the parties to the project will have what they need on a timely basis in order to achieve the success of the project. These rules include response time, clarity, integrity, and respectfully honoring each other as partners. They make the process easier, smoother, and more enjoyable.

Once the rules have been established, it is necessary to lay out in no uncertain terms the promised considerations in the form of recognition and reward the partners will receive once their project has been successfully completed. This will avoid any question about who gets what so as not to undermine the project. Reward and recognition are generators of repeat business, referrals, and longer-term relationships. Lastly, define the consequences of both success and failure. Consequences, simply put, are the outcomes that result from action or inaction. Consequences can be either positive or negative. Map out clearly and specifically the consequences that will result if the project is completed on time, or earlier, and complies with the agreed upon guidelines and commitments, and if it does not.

What You Can Do

In order to fully develop the natural skills these three modules are designed to bring out, there are actions you can take to ensure that happens with velocity, certainty, and power. The first challenge is to memorize the names of the modules, the names of the practices, and the names of the steps of each practice until you know them like you know your name. The next step is to learn what each module, practice, and step does. By learning, I mean memorize. This is the less glamorous part of the ASM. Yet, without it, you'll fail to recognize the steps when you see them, making it more difficult to see how they work and delaying your ability to begin executing them intentionally.

These steps are valuable in any selling conversation, whether as a professional seller or in some other role you play. So, begin to practice the steps in *every* conversation you have. Evoke rapport, generate projects, and forge partnership with family members, co-workers, or the cashier at the store. It is important to build this skill one conversation at a time. From a professional standpoint, you can create a practice script that follows the steps of each practice in each module using either a hypothetical or a real client. Practice reading your script aloud several times a day. Having practiced on your own, what then works best is to find a partner you can work with and roleplay your practice script a number of times a week, getting input from your partner along the way. Never use your practice script in actual conversations.

There isn't a single human being without a project. Everyone wants to get somewhere they are not currently. You can practice being interested in others and their projects any time you engage with another person, asking where they'd like to get to and why. With your clients, start taking more of an interest in finding out about them; switch from "get" mode to "give" mode. And just like everyone having a project, everyone has circumstances, or factors, that are potentially in the way of them getting to where they want to go. Start asking people (clients especially) what could get in the way of them achieving their vision. Notice when you start to take center stage and step back into the wings. Don't be afraid to dig deep. The client who says they want more money surely has some vision about what they might do with it.

Likewise, the person who says that they want to retire may need a plan for what they will do with their time and financial resources once that happens. Your job as a trusted advisor is to clarify how they will create that future.

Having a deal completion process to follow allows us to rise above our resistance to completing things.

Chapter Nine
Executing Completion
The Final Three Modules of the Advisory Selling Method

I t is one thing to get a deal into existence and an entirely different thing to get it completed successfully. In order to ensure that a client project gets completed on time and in the best possible manner, it is essential to manage client accountability. It can be a significant challenge to keep the client on track to their own success, especially when the advisor is unclear on how to apply the language of accountability or doesn't know it at all.

Get the Deal Process
Completed

Module 6	**Completing Projects**	Regulator
Module 5	**Creating Breakthroughs**	Operator
Module 4	**Managing Accountability**	Generator

Advisory Selling Modules for
Executing Completion

Now that you have a deal in the works, there are three modules that will ensure full deal completion. The Managing Accountability module is designed to get a deal back on track when it begins to go off track. Creating Breakthroughs empowers the advisor to support the client to get unstuck when they are stuck in their thinking. And Completing Projects offers a way to generate repeat business, referrals, and great recommendations once the project has been realized.

Module 4: Managing Accountability

The fourth module focuses on managing accountability. In this module you learn how to ensure that commitments made are commitments kept. This is the single most influential factor in sustaining a partnership between advisors and clients. The source of all human power is our innate ability to make commitments and keep them. The biggest challenge is knowing how to only make commitments you can keep, and keeping the ones you make. The three practices of this module are Establishing Alignment, Initiating Actions, and Reaffirming Commitments.

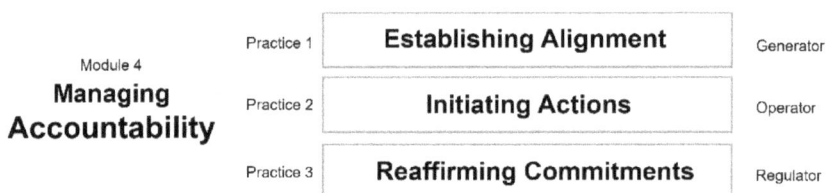

Module 4	Practice 1	**Establishing Alignment**	Generator
Managing Accountability	Practice 2	**Initiating Actions**	Operator
	Practice 3	**Reaffirming Commitments**	Regulator

When you break a commitment with a client, you weaken the relationship. When they break a commitment with you, the relationship is likewise weakened. When you break a commitment with yourself, you weaken your relationship with yourself, causing you to lose power. Therefore, managing accountability is crucial in order to prevent broken commitments and the damage they cause. Failure to do so puts any deal process at risk and minimizes the likelihood of building a long-term productive relationship with a client.

Practice 1: Establishing Alignment

In order to establish alignment, first listen to and embrace a client's assessment of their situation, whether or not that assessment is consistent with the facts. All assessments to some degree are based on assumptions the client has made and rarely based only on the actual facts of their current situation. These assumptions are their personal interpretations of their past experiences and color their view of the future in a way that may lead them to believe what isn't true, limiting their ability to take appropriate action. Your job with this practice is to displace the assumptions of the client with the facts of the situation and to do it without making them or their assessment wrong so that a battle over who is right and who is wrong does not happen. This can be risky business. However, it is the only way to establish alignment with the client so that they embrace an accurate assessment of their situation.

Practice 1			
	Step 1	**Assessment**	Lead
Establishing Alignment	Step 2	**Assumptions**	Ground
	Step 3	**Alignment**	Key
	Step 4	**Assertion**	Offer
	Step 5	**Accountability**	Transition

Once alignment on the accurate assessment has been achieved, the advisor asserts a best course of action for the client and generates alignment with them in regard to that course. Finally, both you and the client will need to determine who will be accountable for each appropriate action necessary to moving the deal process forward toward completion. Said another way, this means making clear who is going to do what and when. Failure to establish alignment on the accurate assessment, the best course of action, and who will be accountable for which actions means accountability will never be strong, and a deal will be at risk.

Practice 2: Initiating Actions

Once you have established alignment with the client, you are positioned to make an effective invitation to act. This invitation to action must be to a specific individual or it will not produce a result. It is imperative to make clear the intention behind the actions so that the client understands how these actions serve their best interest. With the intention clarified, the advisor lays out in very specific objective terms the actions necessary to completing the client project so that there is no question as to what is needed and no chance of a misunderstanding by the client. To avoid the great risk of actions not being done on time, include a precise date and time for each action to be initiated and completed. The point is to significantly lessen the chances of a client breaking a commitment.

Practice 2 Initiating Action	Step	Action	Role
	Step 1	**Intention**	Lead
	Step 2	**Action**	Ground
	Step 3	**Date/Time**	Key
	Step 4	**Invitation**	Offer
	Step 5	**Commitment**	Transition

Using the steps above, invite the client (an individual not a group) to take compelling actions on their project. An effective invitation is very clear. If any of the above three components is not spoken or spoken incompletely, the client will go on the defensive and blame the advisor for their own mistake. The recipient of the invitation has four initial options available to them in response to your invitation. The first is to accept. This means they are promising to comply with the request. The second option is to decline. By declining, they are promising not to comply with the request.

The third possibility is that they may counter with a requested adjustment of actions or timing. This is usually the best-case scenario, because when a counter is offered, it shows that the client is thinking and not blindly setting themselves up for a broken commitment. The fourth option is sometimes necessary if the client is unable to respond to your invitation at the time it is made. This is called a defer. When a client defers, they are not in a position to make a commitment without taking the time to examine their situation and their capability of making said commitment.

Over time, it may become clear that a commitment made cannot be kept. At this point you need to invite the client to revoke their commitment and make a new one. Staying out ahead of a client breaking their commitment to you, empowers you, the client, and the project itself and mitigates the risk of the client blaming you for what they did not do.

Practice 3: Reaffirming Commitments

What makes human beings powerful is the ability to say what we are going to do and do it. Making commitments is a function of human spirit. Breaking them, and justifying why, are the mechanisms of human nature. Since everyone is part human spirit and part human nature, they have a hard time making and keeping commitments to themselves and others, leaving most people with broken commitments in the past. When they make yet another commitment on top of their history of broken promises, the new commitment must be reaffirmed. The greatest risk comes into play when an invitation has been accepted. Broken commitments in the past leave people with a loss of power. Your job is to empower the client by managing them and their relationship to their commitments. This practice helps clients take ownership of keeping their commitments, which could otherwise easily slip through the cracks.

	Step 1	**Reflect**	Lead
	Step 2	**Reopen**	Ground
Practice 3 **Reaffirming Commitments**	Step 3	**Reconcile**	Key
	Step 4	**Remedy**	Offer
	Step 5	**Reaffirm**	Transition

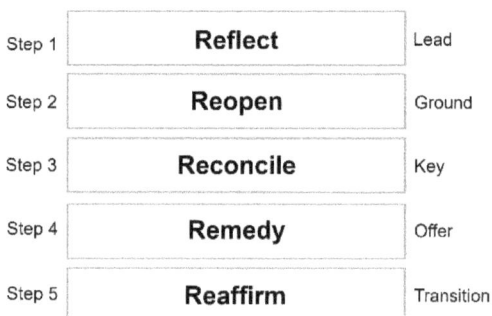

When a person breaks a commitment, they become a perpetrator, and like most perpetrators, they must justify their mistake or lack of action. To do this, they invalidate their relationship with the person against whom they perpetrated by making up a negative story about that person, one which contains very few facts. If you allow a client to break a promise with you, they will find a way to make you wrong for their mistake. This means whenever a client breaks a promise, you pay the price. Doing this enough times will cause a client-advisor partnership to slowly deteriorate and ultimately dissolve if left unchecked and not managed. It's your job as the trusted advisor to provide the leadership the client needs to rise above their own self-defeating behavior.

The first rule for reaffirming commitments is to never make a commitment you can't keep and keep the ones you make. The second is to never let a client break a commitment. This requires staying ahead of their potential broken commitments at all costs. As a trusted advisor, it is imperative that you be always vigilant about making and keeping your commitments to clients. Even more so, you must be vigilant about ensuring that the client keeps the commitments they have made to you. Failure to do this puts the relationship and the project at risk.

Reaffirming a commitment looks like this. At any time during the deal process, you may begin to reflect on whether or not you can trust the client to keep one or more of their commitments. Or it may become absolutely clear that a commitment the client made cannot be kept. Perhaps there is a pattern of broken commitments already. When this happens, the advisor needs to reopen the Advisory Selling conversation, asking a question such as, "Is there anything that could keep this from happening?" Then work with the client to reconcile how any obstacle that may emerge can be dealt with so that it does not interfere with the client keeping the commitment and invite them to revoke their previous commitment and make a new one.

The next step is to put into place some further remedy that will ensure that anything else that comes up can be dealt with through communication between the advisor and client. Finally, reaffirm the client's commitment so that they becomes a full partner in making sure that their commitment will be fulfilled by the date and time specified.

Module 5: Creating Breakthroughs

Breakdowns create breakthroughs. There is no such thing as a breakthrough that's not preceded by a breakdown. A breakdown is the opening of a doorway to a new reality, but only if we have the ability to see it that way. It is important to learn how to be empowered by breakdowns. Every major champion in any sport is a champion only because they understand how to be empowered by defeat, coming back stronger than ever before. Every breakdown can bring you to the bottom of the next level of performance. This is redemption, and that's what creating breakthroughs is all about.

Sometimes, in the course of the deal process, a client may get stuck in their thinking, and it becomes imperative for the trusted advisor to get the client unstuck. So many deals blow up in a selling agent's face because they are unequipped to deal with clients when they get stuck. These three practices together are the remedy. They are akin to a civil war battlefield surgeon first cutting the skin of a wounded soldier (talking straight), reaching in and taking out the bullet (drilling down), then patching up the wound (rebuilding trust). This is rarely a pleasant experience for the client or advisor but may, at times, be necessary if a deal is going to proceed to a successful completion.

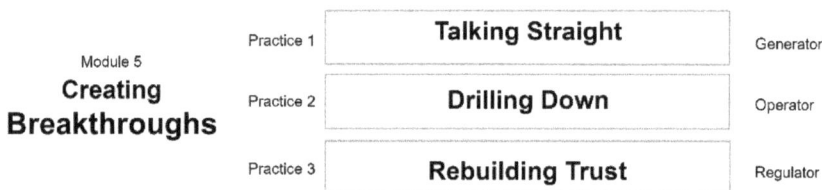

	Practice 1	**Talking Straight**	Generator
Module 5 **Creating** **Breakthroughs**	Practice 2	**Drilling Down**	Operator
	Practice 3	**Rebuilding Trust**	Regulator

Clients can fall into denial, deception, and delusion and become stuck in inaction. The trusted advisor's job, using the practices of this module, is to cut through client delusion which is a product of their denial and deception. Their denial shows up when they deny the facts of their situation. Deception takes hold when what they claim to others is different from the facts. But the most damaging impact is when clients buy into the lies they've told, as if they are true. This is their delusion.

Denial, deception, and delusion are the downfall of human beings. The Talking Straight practice cuts through denial. The Drilling Down practice exposes the deception so that there's no place to hide. The third practice, Rebuilding Trust, opens a doorway for the client to escape the trap of their delusion thus setting themselves, and you, free.

This is more like surgery than selling. Denial, deception, and delusion form the basic human addictive pattern. An alcoholic will claim that they are not seriously affected by alcohol. They will tell others that they actually function better with alcohol. They begin to believe the lies they tell and drown themselves in drink. The worst part of this basic human pattern of ineffectiveness is that we buy into the lies we tell, which becomes our deluded reality from which inappropriate and ineffective choices stem. Advisors must have the courage to intervene in the process of clients drinking their own Kool-Aid and talking themselves down the tube.

Practice 1: Talking Straight

Creating breakthroughs for clients requires a level of straight talk which most people shy away from. As an advisor, you don't have that luxury. You have to dig deep into your commitment to the client and their project to find the courage to perform the needed "surgery." It is likely to be painful. First you have to elicit from the client their fantasy about their situation, whether positive or negative, that has them entangled and, possibly, deluded and is shaping their actions in a way that becomes more and more counterproductive. The next step is to expose the client's fear that is at the source of their fantasy, and that has been festering, so that the client can face it, embrace it, and cut through whatever denial, deception, and delusion that fear has been feeding.

Practice 1 **Talking Straight**	Step 1	**Fantasy**	Lead
	Step 2	**Fear**	Ground
	Step 3	**Facts**	Key
	Step 4	**Truth**	Offer
	Step 5	**Freedom**	Transition

It is important to support the client in seeing how their interpretations of the facts about their situation have distorted their thinking. Once they are able to observe the facts more clearly, they will come to see the truth as a basis of their future choices and will move their project forward. The truth usually makes people angry, The advisor must allow the client to be upset upon learning the truth. Their upset is an integral part of the transformation that must take place if a person is ever going to accomplish their project. From here, the advisor encourages the client's new sense of freedom to move their project forward as the truth continues to do its work on them once the truth has become clear and the lie has been pushed aside.

When people hear the truth, they get angry. It's not something that can be avoided, it's part of our human nature. Yet it is rarely comfortable. The truth also has the power to give one freedom, because once it's been spoken, there is nowhere else to go, nowhere to hide. This process may take two hours, two days, two weeks, two months, or two years, but the truth brought to light will do its work to heal the damage caused by the lie. Once this work is complete, trusted advisors and clients can rebuild a productive partnership.

Practice 2: Drilling Down

To ensure that a breakthrough in thinking becomes more sustainable for a client, you must drill down further to squeeze out any remaining denial so only the truth is exposed. Any remaining denial will fester like a battlefield wound left unattended. It is important to confront a client with what will be required of them if they are to have any hope of completing their project. Any residual deception will eat away at the partnership Drilling down and confronting a client at a deeper level makes it possible to challenge the client to see if they are willing to do what it takes to rethink their situation and take corrective actions. This practice removes any trace of delusion with surgical precision. Like with any major operation, Advisory Selling conversations at this level put the client relationship at high risk. In order to reduce the risk of compromising the relationship, we must repair any damage that may have been incurred.

Practice 2 **Drilling Down**	Step 1	**Observe**	Lead
	Step 2	**Question**	Ground
	Step 3	**Challenge**	Key
	Step 4	**Confront**	Offer
	Step 5	**Demand**	Transition

To do that, the advisor works with the client now that they are no longer limited by their fantasy and helps them to observe the facts of their situation fully, laying out a plan of action for how to move their project forward. Next, squeeze out any last drops of denial, deception, and delusion that may cause the problem to reemerge by questioning the client's commitment. This means confronting the client to see if they are truly ready to get back on track and take responsibility for doing their part in ensuring their success. To really drive the point home, the advisor needs to challenge the client as to whether or not they now have the commitment needed to move forward with velocity, in full partnership with the advisor, and win their game. The final step in the Drilling Down practice is to lay out a list of specific demands that the client must fulfill if they are to reengage and ramp up to the level needed to get their job done.

Practice 3: Rebuilding Trust

Because Advisory Selling breakthrough conversations are extremely difficult, the partnership is at risk of falling apart. Having opened up a wound by talking straight and drilling down, the advisor now uses this practice to patch up the wound so that the advisor-client relationship grows stronger than it was before the conversation took place. To start this process, the advisor reviews with the client the facts of what happened and each of them must take responsibility for their mistakes that led to the breakdown in thinking or action. The advisor takes responsibility for the mistake they made of not leading the client in a manner that would have avoided client mistakes and the impact of those mistakes in order to get the client to take responsibility for their own mistakes.

	Step 1	**Review**	Lead
	Step 2	**Responsibility**	Ground
Practice 3			
Rebuilding	Step 3	**Reconcile**	Key
Trust	Step 4	**Remedy**	Offer
	Step 5	**Redeem**	Transition

Once both advisor and client have taken responsibility for their mistakes, reconcile any damage between advisor and client making sure not to devolve into fault, shame, blame, or guilt. The next step is to create a remedy, with the client, that will ensure that these mistakes are not only not repeated in the future but one that would make dealing with any other mistakes less challenging to the advisor-client relationship. Finally, the advisor conveys to the client that there is an opportunity for the partnership, as a result of the breakdown, to become stronger and more fulfilling than it could have ever been. This entire process, when executed properly, not only redeems the damaged relationship, but builds one that is more valued and enduring than before. This act of rebuilding trust opens a doorway for the client to escape the trap of their delusion, get back on track with the partnership, and move forward once again toward the completion of their project.

Module 6 - Completing Projects

Now that you have launched a client project, managed accountability each step of the way, and created client breakthroughs, you are in a position to help the client successfully complete their project. At the completion of a transactional process, it is essential to complete it in a manner that is memorable and builds toward repeat business, referrals, and great recommendations going forward.

	Practice 1	**Securing Approvals**	Generator
Module 6			
Completing	Practice 2	**Executing Transactions**	Operator
Projects			
	Practice 3	**Celebrating Completion**	Regulator

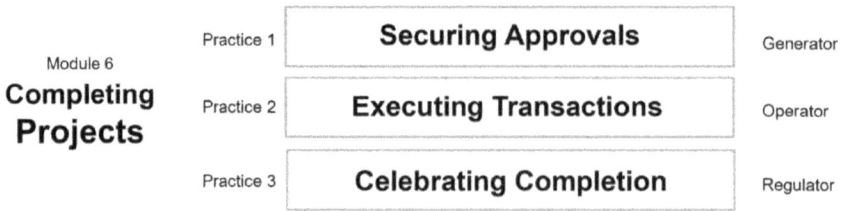

The sixth learning module is Completing Projects and consists of three practices: Securing Approvals, Executing Transactions, and Celebrating Completion. Securing approvals is an art form that must be practiced with precision. Executing transactions must be a special event so there's no question that all parties agree that a project has been successfully completed. Celebrating completion is something many clients and agents ignore at their own peril. Skipping this important step is a sure way to undermine your chances for repeat business and referrals. If you fail to complete clients' projects using these three practices, you miss one of the biggest business generation opportunities ever.

Practice 1: Securing Approvals

Some projects might require getting approvals from one or more entities to be complete. An advisor's job is to work to gather all the necessary data and organize it in a way that will make a case for the approval of the completion of the project. Once gathered, the agent positions this information, using their experience and expertise, so that it is aligned with what is needed to satisfy the approval requirements, clearly showing why the project is ready for completion, thus influencing the process in the desired direction.

	Step 1	**Gathering**	Lead
Practice 1	Step 2	**Positioning**	Ground
Securing	Step 3	**Advocating**	Key
Approvals	Step 4	**Deliberating**	Offer
	Step 5	**Approving**	Transition

By boldly advocating your positioning to all parties involved in the process of designing, executing, and completing the project, then providing adequate time for deliberation, the chances for approval become more certain. Approval, once secured from the client, will naturally lead to the completion of the project in a manner that will build stronger relationships and bring certainty to the process of completing the project.

Practice 2: Executing Transactions

The execution of a transaction is something both advisors and clients would prefer to minimize or avoid because it is a line of demarcation between what is past and what is now a new reality moving into the future. Once the project has been completed, everything is going to change. Such change is difficult for most people to confront, even when it is what they wanted. Therefore, this completion event must be special.

	Step 1	**Staging**	Lead
Practice 2	Step 2	**Delivery**	Ground
Executing	Step 3	**Verifying**	Key
Transactions	Step 4	**Securing**	Offer
	Step 5	**Executing**	Transition

This practice is intended to give form to the completion process. Its purpose is to emphasize the importance of the client's project, the partnership with the advisor, and the results produced. It is essential that you follow a precise protocol. First, you must determine and stage the location of the project completion event. Stage the event such that a complete plan has been formulated and aligned on so that the process of completion can be initiated with confidence. You then need to deliver all the people who have participated in the project along with the necessary materials to the event site. At the time of the event, be sure to verify that everything and everyone is present.

Make certain that any doubts about how the event will be rolled out have been quelled, and that the participants are ready for the execution event. The next step is to put measures in place to secure the space from interruptions or distractions to the culmination of the process, which should be executed with some objective document, such as a contract, agreement, or strategic plan so that it becomes clear to all that this particular project is no longer active. This is what makes the execution of the project completion event noteworthy.

Practice 3: Celebrating Completion

This final practice is key to creating a long-term relationship. To fully complete a project a formal celebration is required. No project is truly finalized unless this crucial practice has been employed. Celebrating completion is best done as an event in which a number of critical actions take place. If agents skip this necessary step, they miss the boat on generating future business.

Practice 3 **Celebrating Completion**	Step 1	Validation	Lead
	Step 2	Recognition	Ground
	Step 3	Appreciation	Key
	Step 4	Recommendation	Offer
	Step 5	Celebration	Transition

The first step is to publicly validate the project or process results produced by the collaboration between the key players, what was done by each person, and what stood out to everyone. Individuals who have contributed to the success of the project should be recognized as those who made important contributions to the outcome of the deal, starting with major players, leaders, and the uniquely skilled people who made the completion of the deal a success. Some sign of appreciation should be given, something that will be valued and remembered.

Make the event more focused on future business and empower enduring relationships with clients. A successful celebration is not only about having a great deal of fun and a real sense of fulfillment, but also an opportunity for both client and trusted advisor to consider what's next in their partnership as well as recommendations and referrals of others who could benefit from the advisor's services. The final phase of a completion event is intended be an outright, uncompromised celebration, no matter how big or small it may be, in which the client and advisor deepen the value of their long-term collaborative relationship.

What You Can Do

The three modules of Executing Completion build on the three from Generating Opportunities. The first set of modules is aimed at bringing an opportunity into existence. This second set is aimed at completing a client project and your transactional process successfully. As with Generating Opportunities, your first task is to memorize the module names, each step, and its function. Once you've got that down, creating scripts for each practice using either a real or hypothetical client, practicing them first by yourself, and then with a roleplay partner, will all serve to accelerate the development of your skills and compress your time frame to achieving consistent high performance.

To be clear, this script is for practice and never to be used in a client conversation. Never! The intention of these scripts is to imitate the steps exactly as written initially. Eventually, as a product of enough regular practice, your conversations will take on your own natural expression. These are your innate skills rising to the surface and integrating into your selling conversations.

When you commit to learning, practicing, and applying all six modules of the Advisory Selling Method, only then will you become skilled at the entire continuum of the selling process and strong enough to fully empower your clients as a trusted advisor. Practicing the skills of the Advisory Selling modules significantly elevates your ability to produce results and build highly productive partnerships with clients.

When a client's project gets accomplished, your client wins. When clients win, you win.

Changing how you sell requires that you risk everything you know. True freedom comes when you step beyond the limits of what you think is true and embrace what is actually true.

Chapter Ten
Changing How You Sell
Taking What You've Learned & Putting It to Work

The key to changing how you sell is to give up being survival-driven and become service-driven. This means letting go of all selling tricks and allowing selling to become the sacred act it was always meant to be. Doing this lifts you out of survival mode to a level of sufficiency, and ultimately, into abundance. There is no more "hurry, scurry, work, and worry," grinding out a living.

Changing how you sell requires taking risks. It is imperative that you be willing to let go of past training and allow your natural Advisory Selling skills to shine through. As you become more familiar with the practices, you begin to see them unfolding in every conversation. Over time, by consistently using these practices, you become more authentic in your interactions with others, letting go of the need to posture, pretend, pitch, promote, or prove your value. Each section of this chapter is a framework designed to develop and bring forth your natural selling skills and guide you in your process of learning the Advisory Selling Method.

Critical Actions to Be Taken

Change might be difficult because it involves taking responsibility for embracing the following actions to change how you sell:

1. Treat clients as fellow human beings, not prey. Stop hunting and fishing from the perspective of "eat what you kill."

2. Shift from the "get" mode of selling to the "give" mode.

3. Expand beyond your comfort zone of focusing on the transaction side of a client relationship and shift the focus to the human side of the selling equation.

4. Break your addiction to the agenda-based tactics, triggers, techniques, tricks, and traps you have accumulated.

5. Manage what you say and make the shift from talking things down the tube to speaking the truth in every conversation. This doesn't always mean being positive; it means speaking powerfully.

6. Become more authentic in your language and actions by shifting away from being aggressive, aversive, apathetic, and overly attentive.

7. Shift away from inductive, deductive, reductive, and seductive modes of selling so you naturally become more eductive and bring out the best in yourself and your clients.

8. Stop showboating to prove your worth. Instead, pull back to the sideline, grab your clients from the stands, and place them squarely onto the field as players.

9. Schedule time daily to intentionally focus on breaking your entrenched agenda-based habits and develop your natural commitment-based skills.

10. Shift from operating out of your default ingrained, survival-driven methods of competition, conspiracy, conflict, and corruption to consciously performing from a human spirit-driven

commitment to creativity, collaboration, compassion, and contribution.

11. Abandon deceptive selling and embrace the challenges of inceptive selling.

12. Follow the five core principles of Advisory Selling: Authentic Commitment, Genuine Interest, Complete Openness, Fearless Communication, Unstoppable Intention.

The following three models are meant to deepen your learning process and accelerate your transition from being a survival-driven agent to a service-driven advisor.

Five Pillars of High Performance

The following five pillars of high performance need to be adopted and practiced in order to further master Advisory Selling.

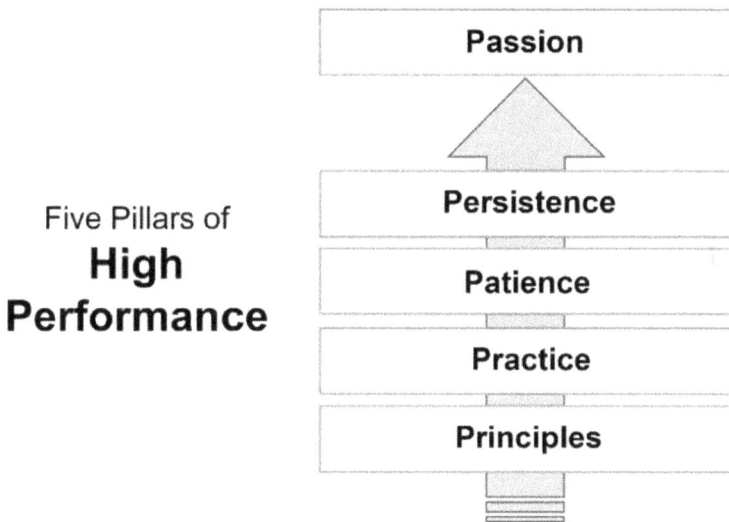

Five Pillars of
**High
Performance**

Passion

Persistence

Patience

Practice

Principles

Principles

The dark force of deceptive selling is always waiting to emerge when there is a confrontation with a client who is too big, too tough, or too deceptive in their own approach. By mastering the five core principles of Advisory Selling, you naturally resist the pull of agenda-based deceptive selling habits from within yourself and from others. These principles are authentic commitment, genuine interest, complete openness, fearless communication, and unstoppable intention. Without such principles as a foundation, the normal drift toward agenda-based selling will seduce you away from commitment-based inceptive selling back into the grip of deceptive selling.

Practice

Mastering the "practice of practice" is vital to achieving a high level of performance in any endeavor. High level performers not only practice to strengthen their weaknesses, they continuously practice the things they have mastered so they don't regress. A commitment to specified practice times, rigorously adhered to, is the foundation on which true championship performance is built. To master your natural Advisory Selling Skills, you need to install a structure for continuous practice.

Patience

Patience is the key to practice, and practice is key to high performance. By mastering patience we are able to endure the frustration of remaining on the sideline. Without the mastery of patience our survival-driven agenda-based habits compel us to storm the field pushing the client back into the stands. The agent can no longer act as the advisor when they attempt to "play the game." They lose the ability to command when they try to control. When this happens, the agent needs to return to the sideline and resume their role as the advisor. The ball must be returned to the client so they can win their game. When clients win, agents, as advisors, also win.

Persistence

Once you master patience, it becomes imperative to master persistence; they go hand in hand. No matter how much you feel you have learned something, it is essential to continuously improve. The choice is clear. Persist in your quest for improvement or fall back to a point from which you may never recover. Selling agents get trapped when they only maintain their level of performance because stabilization leads to stagnation. Hence the saying: the seeds of our demise are planted in the good times. For champions there is no resting on laurels, there is only continuous improvement.

Passion

Passion is the ultimate quality of a champion. If you are not passionate about what you are doing, you will never be good at it. Passion is something generated from within oneself, not something acquired from others or your circumstances. Without passion, there is no drive for mastery. In any sport, the best player and best teams are always the ones that express their passion by adhering to their core principles, practicing regularly, preparing before every game, presenting their best on the playing field, and producing results that exceed expectations.

Knowledge into Application

The Advisory Selling Method provides a structured approach in which you can apply your knowledge to produce significant results even with limited practice time. To become trusted advisors, selling agents must learn to shift from "winging it" to delivering services based on consistent practice. Unlike actors and athletes who spend 95% of their time preparing and practicing, agents cannot dedicate that much time. However, if you were to dedicate just 5% of your time to practice, it would equate to 30 minutes a day in a 50-hour week.

A solid approach to developing your Advisory Selling Skills is accomplished by moving through the following phases in sequence:

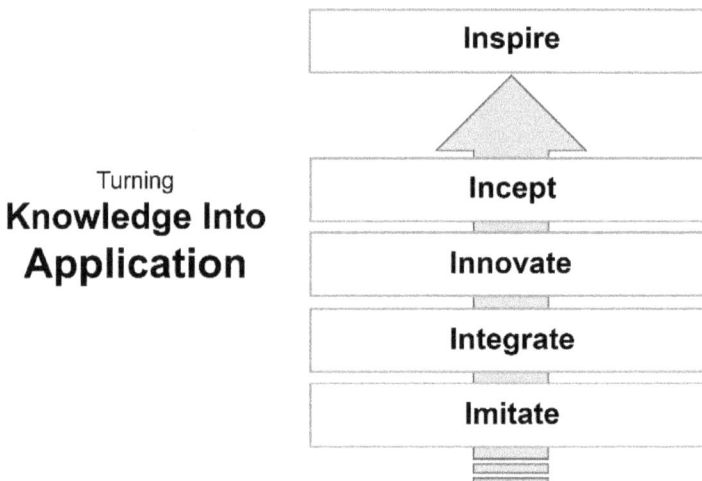

Imitate

It is necessary to follow the practices of the Advisory Selling Method exactly as you would follow a martial arts teacher in their class. This is especially important when developing your inner commitment-based skills. Martial arts teachers practice for decades and work diligently to replicate the exact same moves they learned from their teacher, gaining in mastery as they grow in precision. By repeatedly imitating the practices, they come more readily, laying a track that can be further developed. The Advisory Selling Method offers a precise principle-based system of modular learning that will bring out the best in you if you simply follow the moves as taught.

Integrate

Once you develop the ability to imitate the teachings, you can begin to make them your own. Each of us is very different, so the inevitable result of imitation will be integration into a form that's uniquely yours. Integration also means that your practice does not disrupt your schedule but becomes an essential part of everything you do. When you learn the Advisory Selling Method, it becomes a permanent part of who you are and how you communicate. It is already within you, waiting to be brought forth and mastered.

Innovate

In every client conversation, you will need to innovate in the moment, because, despite how much practice you may have, real client conversations rarely follow the practice model. Today's client conversation will not be the same as yesterday's conversation. Since we live in a chaotic universe, everything changes all the time. People change from day to day, hour to hour, and moment to moment. Your practice should be strong enough that your delivery can be effective in a moment of need. Clients judge agents not so much on their content as they do on their delivery. They can usually tell if you are an agenda-based selling agent or commitment-based advisor. When you are agenda-based in your approach, clients will fight back with their own agenda. This leads to warring agendas that will never establish partnership and inevitably results in some disadvantage to the agent.

To avoid this conflict of agendas, you need to develop your ability to innovate in the moment in response to unpredictable client challenges. Innovation means to "make-up" a new way of doing the same thing, like taking the same three-point shot in a different way depending on the circumstances. Without mastery of innovation there can be no victory. Mastery requires practice. Without practice you will end up faking it like most agenda-based selling agents are forced to do in the absence of a method. The disciplined practice of the Advisory Selling Method will seem like you are imposing constraints. In truth, those "constraints" are the pathway to greater freedom to master the challenge of innovating in the moment.

Incept

In the pursuit of your natural Advisory Selling Skills, having mastered innovation, you must practice the art of inception and abandon deception. The pervasive influence of agenda-based deception in our human culture makes learning commitment-based inception more challenging. Like most of us, clients are beset with deep self-doubt, whether consciously or unconsciously. The art of inceptive selling infuses clients with a spirit of commitment, clarity, confidence, and courage which they will need in order to take significant action. Developing your capacity to incept an idea within a client that will blossom and grow to empower them and those around them to make smart choices is what Advisory Selling is all about.

Inspire

Because most of us only have a vague notion of what we want in the future, we are not often inspired. Ultimately, it is the trusted advisor's job to inspire clients to see a future worth pursuing and help them get excited about getting there. Agents, as advisors, compel clients to take actions that, as challenging as they may be, are what serve the clients' best interests and the fulfillment of their visions. People don't simply pay for a product, service, or asset. In truth, they pay for the future that product, service, or asset will make possible for them. We're all on an endless search for ways to get from where we are to where we want to be. We get inspired when we see that future and how to get there, clearly and fully.

Roadmap to Learning

To face the challenge of altering your inherited, acquired, and developed DNA of selling, it takes a measure of commitment many have never shown before. In order to do this, you have to pass through the gauntlet of your normal learning process to achieve a new clarity and a new reality you may have never previously known. There are five levels you need to negotiate in order to accomplish this.

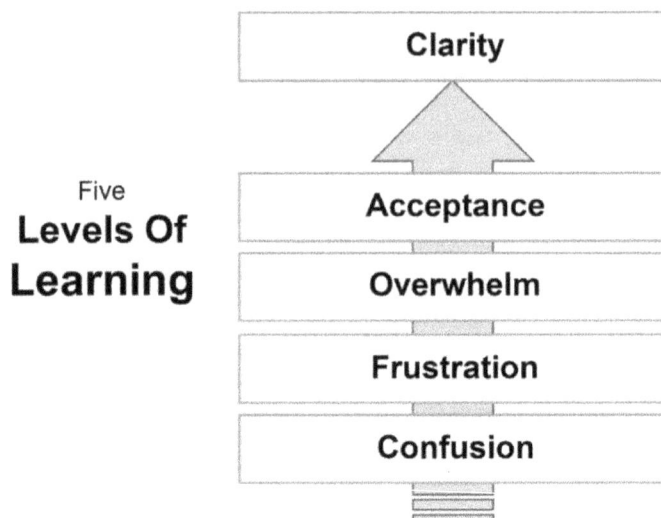

Five
**Levels Of
Learning**

Clarity

Acceptance

Overwhelm

Frustration

Confusion

Confusion

When encountering confusion, many people stop in their tracks be-cause they fear confronting the zone of "not knowing." Confusion, in terms of skill development, means not understanding how to do some-thing. Facing this obstacle can be daunting since you must embrace the idea that there is something you have never fully considered before. (If you are confused by this, you're in the right place.) Mastering the art of not knowing what to do or how to do something means mastering your ability to "not know" and continue to move forward in the face of complete uncertainty.

Frustration

As you pursue learning new skills and begin to get a sense of how some-thing is done, another obstacle to learning presents itself. This is called frustration. Frustration means that you may know how to do some-thing but can't do it very well. Facing up to being lousy at something isn't comfortable, but it is necessary to continue to pursue your commitment to learning. Facing a significant need for improvement often takes people out of the learning game and prevents them from ever achieving a new reality. If you can embrace your need for improvement and the frustration that comes with it, you will see that getting good at something is possible.

Overwhelm

Experiencing overwhelm should be encouraging because, at this point, you know how to do something and you can do it fairly well. However, there is so much to do beyond what you think you can handle. The feeling of overwhelm is a higher level in the learning process and a true sign that you now have some likelihood of success. You are at a turning point and a line of demarcation from which there is no return.

Instead of being seduced by the allure of multitasking and multiple distractions, it is imperative that you tackle one thing at a time in order to avoid becoming scattered. The best way to deal with being overwhelmed is to pick one thing and focus on completing it before moving on to the next. You will quickly rise above the overwhelm and arrive at the next level, which is acceptance.

Acceptance

Once we know how to do something, can do it well, and get it all done, we still fall short. On the pathway to mastery, there is no arrival. There can only be acceptance. Some people stop here and allow their emotional response to get the best of them. They fall back into complaining about the overwhelm and that they will never be good at the new skill, or anything else for that matter. Unfortunately, despite being so close to the clarity we seek, we stop learning, because the discomfort of con-fusion, frustration, and overwhelm becomes intolerable. At this point we must embrace the possibility that what we want to achieve cannot be accomplished. It is not so much about giving up as it is about being willing to accept that something may never happen. Most people are conditioned to hesitate to cross this line to fight for what they want. But extraordinary people never hesitate to face the new ground zero where they give up all hope and surrender to the truth of what is so. This moment of acceptance of ultimate defeat opens the door to the clarity necessary to achieving complete success. Only when full ac-ceptance is embraced can we then step across the threshold into the realm of clarity.

Clarity

Clarity is a dangerous point to reach. It puts you at the greatest risk. It is at this stage that you are most likely to stop learning because you assume that since you know something so well, you've reached the final destination. This mindset hinders any further development of your skills. Clarity often leads to complacency, where you become a "know-it-all" and no longer question. Complacency can only be overcome through continuous learning. Champion athletes understand that to maintain their champion status, they must never cease practicing what they have already mastered. They constantly strive to look beyond and discover deeper dimensions in their field. Even in a state of clarity, one should never let complacency undermine continued learning. While you may have entered a new reality, it's important to remember that you are on a journey that should never end.

To ensure your journey continues, you must take responsibility for learning, practicing, and applying the principles of Advisory Selling in all possible situations with clients and colleagues. Through consistent effort, you will find your voice, allowing your natural skills to emerge, take over, unfold, and become your dominant way of being.

If you find that you are not fully grasping the five levels of learning, it's a positive sign because being honest with yourself about your limitations is an excellent first step. By following the teachings presented in this book, you will progress toward understanding them. I am confident in the existence of the reality I describe because I live it, and I can't wait for you to join me the there.

Creating a Game Worth Winning

Changing how you sell changes everything. This requires acknowledging that you are fully capable of making this change. I am committed to helping you develop your natural skills and maximize your performance in the best way possible. This does require work, especially if you are already successfully using other previously learned selling strategies. I invite you to begin your process of transitioning from your normal agenda-based selling habits to the full expression of your innate commitment-based Advisory Selling skills. I promise everything being offered will give you significant advantages for accomplishing this regardless of the challenges you're facing.

By changing how you sell, clients and colleagues will also change how they sell. Changing who you are being does not mean becoming another person; it means being truer to yourself and shedding the accumulated bad habits and negative behaviors that are always present in all our lives. If you are anything like me, you have a vision of changing the world for the better. Transforming this vision into a reality only happens when people change how they sell, in turn, changing the world as we know it. Changing the world requires that we first change ourselves and then encourage others to do the same.

There is nothing you need to do except to shift from the compromises you have made in your attempt to get what you want to focusing on being of service to others. It always turns out, the more we contribute to the wellbeing and success of others, the more we find our own success and fulfillment beyond what we could ever have previously hoped to achieve.

You already have within you everything you need. Searching for answers outside of yourself will drain your power. You are fully capable of bringing out your natural Advisory Selling skills, just like many others have done before you. Remember, you can access the magic of the Advisory Selling Method in the following ways:

- o   If you know the practices, you will see them unfold before you in every Advisory Selling conversation.

- o   When you take time to hone the practices, you will bring out your natural inner skills in their full power.

- o   If you consistently apply the practices over time, you will transform who you are being, your relationships with others, and the world around you.

Once you develop this new capacity to pursue the learning process, you achieve an entirely new level of generating money. Money is the currency of accomplishment and fulfillment. You become a person who leans toward creativity, collaboration, compassion, and contribution, and therefore become more consequential, deftly outmaneuvering competition, conspiracy, conflict, and corruption whenever they emerge.

We now have an opportunity to turn selling into a pursuit of fulfillment in life by serving the best interests of others. As stated at the beginning of this book, every person is selling something to someone all the time, including to themselves. We cannot escape selling because it is the primary characteristic that makes us human. By selling the truth using the Advisory Selling Method, your clients win and you win too.

Nothing could be more important than changing how you sell because mastering our most critical human skill – selling – is essential to being an accomplished, fulfilled, and effective human being. I invite you to change how you sell and I promise that if you do, everything in your life will change.

What I am suggesting may be easy in description but more challenging in execution. I will not wish you the best of luck because it isn't about luck at all. Instead, I am wishing you to be your best in every way. Once you get to that place, there will be no turning back.

Welcome to the brave new world of Advisory Selling.

Real learning only happens when you take the time to fully acknowledge to yourself and others what you have learned.

CONCLUSION
ADVISORY SELLING REVIEW
Own What You Have Learned and Put It to Work

This book is in no way meant to minimize what you already know is working for you. And, it has taken you into new territory when it comes to selling. By reading this book, you gave me permission to enter your private world and introduce new ideas that could shake up that world. My interest is in you and what relationship we can build over the long-term. The knowledge you have gained will only have power if you apply it consistently over time, because knowledge unapplied makes no difference. The questions to ask yourself are "What did you get out of this book, and how are you going to use it?"

We have covered a lot of ground, spanning the origins and evolution of selling through the different styles, modes, and ways of selling to better understand the principles, practices, and process of Advisory Selling. Change is always challenging, even if you are eager to make it happen. This is especially challenging when changing the long established and commonly accepted language habits you have used to survive and achieve success thus far. If you are to take selling to a new level of consistent performance improvement, you must begin to uncover the natural selling skills hidden within you that are aching to come out and be put to work.

Advisory Selling offers an important innovation that empowers agents, managers, and executives to become trusted advisors by discarding the traditional tactics, techniques, triggers, tricks, and traps used to manipulate clients and customers. It allows anyone to transcend the limits of deceptive agenda-based selling, let go of their addiction to getting what they want at the client's expense, and to stop the endless search for new victims. When fully applied, this method changes how you sell so that you are using your natural skills at selling the truth as your dominant mode of connecting with clients. This allows you to let go of your reliance on cheap tricks and allow selling to become the sacred act selling was always meant to be, enabling you to be the truest version of yourself, a person who places being of service to others at the forefront.

Having explored the history, evolution, repercussions, and rewards of various selling methods, let's revisit each chapter's core message to help to anchor your new knowledge, repetition being one of the key tenets of learning. The chapters in the book are intentionally organized to give you a big picture view of selling before taking a deeper dive into the specifics of the Advisory Selling Method. What follows is a review of the territory covered and what you've accomplished along the way.

Introduction

Changing How You Sell

To be clear, reinventing does not mean replacing. It simply means getting to the core of what selling has always been rather than presenting a new set of techniques and tricks for selling lies to your clients. You learned that, at its core, selling the truth is sacred and should be approached with great regard for those receiving your services. Reinventing, in this context, does not make something new but rather, it makes something that is true to what it was always meant to be.

Part I: Why We Sell & Breaking From the Past

The Origins & Evolution of Selling

Chapter 1: Natural Born Sellers

Everyone Is Always Selling Something

The first new idea you learned is that everyone is selling all the time and there is no escape. In this chapter, we explored how we are all natural born sellers and that every conversation had by every person is unavoidably a selling conversation.

You were introduced to Seven Levels of Being. This continuum flows from the weakest version of being human to the strongest. You can choose who you will be in every area of your life every moment of every day. A person's relationship to who they are being is indicated at each level. Inside this paradigm, a wimp thinks they know everything, and the master is peacefully aware that they know nothing at all. Changing how you sell will require you to step up to Player, risk being the Fool, and ultimately become a Champion.

- o **Wimp** – Never bothers to complain and has an answer for why everything in life isn't working

- o **Victim** – Complains about how others and circumstances are to blame and thinks they know a lot

- o **Bozo** – Pretends to be doing everything that is required but isn't and thinks they know enough

- o **Player** – Willing to produce at least the minimum benchmarks of activity and knows something

- o **Fool** – Willing to step out and risk failing again and again and realizes they don't know as much as they thought

- o **Champion** – A fool who continues to risk, blows it, but then nails it again and again and knows they know little

- o **Master** – A person who steps out and nails it every time while practicing the art of knowing nothing and continuously learning

You also discovered that the world is shaped to some degree by our thinking and actions, but more than anything else, it is shaped by our speaking. Everything we know has been spoken into existence, or more precisely, sold into existence. The world is shaped by what comes out of our mouths. Without this phenomenon, we would still be banging rocks together to make tools. We all have the fundamental choice of how we talk to ourselves, our colleagues, our clients, and our world. We are either selling lies or we are selling the truth. We are either selling Up the Tube or Down the Tube. Unfortunately, despite their accomplishments, many play it safe and choose the downward option.

- o **Up the Tube** – Speaking a positive and productive reality into existence

- o **Down the Tube** – Speaking a negative reality into existence

Chapter 2: Why Selling Began

Origins and Foundations of Selling

In this chapter, you discovered that the origins of selling date back to prehistoric times. Because of our frailty in the face of the overwhelming danger posed by creatures many times our size, and continuous threat to our survival, we invented selling to survive. It was primarily deceptive selling because humans and creatures were in fierce competition to see who could outsmart whom. You also learned that every time you open your mouth to speak, you are confronted with two primary selling choices:

- ○ **Deceptive Selling** – Plant a seed for a fantasy future that may never be achieved or one that may be harmful to a client's best interest and detrimental to others, in order to cash a check

- ○ **Inceptive Selling** – Plant a seed of an idea about a powerful future that will blossom in the client's thinking and, as it unfolds, will serve their best interest and the best interest of everyone they touch

Changing how you sell will require that you learn to distinguish between deceptive selling, selling a lie, and inceptive selling, selling the truth. We will never fully shake off deceptive selling. However, never again does it need to be what limits our relationships with others. The normal habits that we have been using must be incorporated into how we sell the truth or they work against us.

Chapter 3: How Selling Evolved

Agenda-Based & Commitment-Based Selling

You learned about how selling has evolved into four distinct common agenda-based selling strategies and one uncommon commitment-based selling strategy. We all ultimately choose what will become our dominant strategy of selling from the following:

- ○ **Aggressive** – Pressuring clients to take an action

- ○ **Aversive** – Pretending not to be selling

- ○ **Apathetic** – Pretending not to care

- ○ **Attentive** – Pleasing clients to no end

o **Authentic** – Straight Advisory Selling conversation regardless of risk

The authentic commitment-based strategy is best fostered by applying the Advisory Selling Principles. Changing how you sell will require that you learn to adhere to the principles, consistently practice the practices, and use them in every selling conversation. Remember, every conversation is a selling conversation, even those with family, friends, and the cashier at the store.

Part II: How We Sell & Current Selling Challenges
Trading in Adversarial Habits for Advisory Skills

Chapter 4: What Are We Really Selling
Influencing Clients to Take Action

It was revealed that most people may have an idea about what they are selling, but usually have no idea about what a client is actually buying. This incongruity creates a situation where the selling agent needs to resort to bullying, wearing down, shaming, or bribing to get clients to take actions they want the client to take.

The definition of selling is universal regardless of the deceptive or inceptive nature of our approach. Selling means **"Working with clients to create a vision of a future possibility that is compelling enough to change their actions in the present."**

On the spectrum between Deceptive and Inceptive Selling, you employ one of the following five Modes of Influence. Which one you choose will depend on how confronted you are by the circumstances and your confidence in your delivery.

- ○ **Inductive** – To push or threaten people to take action

- ○ **Deductive** – To explain, hoping people will take action

- ○ **Reductive** – To diminish people so they take action

- ○ **Seductive** – To bribe people to get them to take action

- ○ **Eductive** – To bring out commitment to take action

By learning and applying the Advisory Selling Method, you will be choosing the Eductive Mode as your dominant Mode of Influence. Rather than impressing clients with your great ability to perform on their behalf, you shift your focus to bringing out the client's commitment to take responsibility for taking the actions needed to achieve the future they want.

Chapter 5: Breaking Our Selling Habits

Shifting from Adversarial to Advisory Conversations

We begin learning selling at birth and, over the years, we have been taught by five major influencers: parents, teachers, managers, consultants, and trainers. As a result, we developed permanently ingrained agenda-based selling habits that are seemingly impossible to break after years of training. They fall into six categories:

- ○ **Control Tactics** – This approach creates an adversarial relationship and includes Controlling the Conversation, Overcoming Objections, and Hitting "Hot Buttons."

- ○ **Manipulation Tricks** – When we can't control a person, we revert to manipulation by Throwing a Softening Statement, Implying Impending Events, and Deferring to a Higher Power.

- o **Domination Techniques** – When manipulation fails us, we revert to domination. We tell them How to Think, we tell them What to Do, and then we Do a Tie Down.

- o **Intimidation Triggers** – Getting desperate in our quest to influence, we next try to intimidate by Creating Urgency, Forecasting Negative Outcomes, and Setting Artificial Deadlines.

- o **Subjugation Traps** – In selling, these are hallowed closing methods designed to corner a person into taking the actions we want. These include doing a Takeaway, offering an Alternate Choice Trial Close, and then insisting that they Thank Us.

- o **Incarceration** – The final event occurring in normal selling is one from which the client cannot escape. There are three phases of incarceration. First, they sign an agreement that they may or may not fully understand and may or may not serve their best interest. Second, they accept an obligation to "serve a sentence," a period of time within which they will complete the agreement, typically by making payments. Third, they submit to an obligation to pay the required costs and are "willing" to suffer the consequences that are imposed if they fail to honor the terms of the agreement.

Changing how you sell means listening to the words coming out of your mouth and seeing how these agenda-based habits drive your selling conversations down the tube. By learning the Advisory Selling Method, you develop an ability to minimize these habits and allow your natural commitment-based selling skills to become dominant. You never completely lose these deceptive habits, although you may learn to adapt them for a higher purpose. What makes the Advisory Selling Method so powerful is the underlying Modular Learning Architecture. The success of any client conversation relies on three critical practices:

Module 1: Building Partnerships

- Practice 1: Evoking Rapport
- Practice 2: Generating Projects
- Practice 3: Forging Partnership

These advisory selling language skills play a pivotal role in building a strong foundation for a productive and enduring relationship between the advisor and the client.

Chapter 6: Navigating the Sea of Babble

Charting Your Course to a New Way of Selling

We talked about the Sea of Babble, the huge wave of conversations that washes across the planet 24/7. Billions of people are talking, and all of them are selling something to someone all the time. Conversations via media, marketing, and the internet amplify the volume and ferocity of this wave, making it almost impossible to get heard. Most people give up trying.

We explored the five typical ways of selling and a new way that is not as common but is necessary to achieving high-performance results. These include:

- **Conspiratorial Selling** – Hurting clients for my gain
- **Competitive Selling** – Outsmarting clients for my gain
- **Consultative Selling** – Selling a solution for my gain
- **Contract Selling** – Imposing agreements for my gain
- **Collaborative Selling** – Working for shared gain
- **Advisory Selling** – Empower clients for their gain

Changing how you sell means loosening the grip of your inherited, acquired, and developed agenda-based selling mode. Operating in that manner, you are constantly looking to get something for yourself at the expense of others. The Advisory Selling Method is about the client winning, thus shifting the focus to a commitment to serving the client's best interest above all else. When clients win, agents who choose to be the trusted advisor also win.

Part III: What Is Possible & Embracing the Future of Selling

Selling As It Was Always Meant to Be

Chapter 7: Advisory Selling Principles

Serving the Client's Best Interest

In this chapter, you learned that Advisory Selling is a whole new way of selling the truth so that clients are fully served. It seems new even though our innate Advisory Selling Skills are the underlying force behind some successful conversations. We delved into the core principles of Advisory Selling and how they offer an uncompromising commitment to client success, ensuring advisor success.

By using this method, you develop a reliable system for practice and preparation. As previously stated, actors, athletes, and agents are all performers. Actors and athletes dedicate a significant amount of time to practicing their craft and preparing for performance. However, agents do not. Agents do not. Many agents, focused solely on performance, use their clients for practice. This can be an expensive habit. When agents commit to taking even minimal time to practice, they need a highly developed method such as the Advisory Selling Method.

The ASM offers a combination of principles, practices, and processes that will empower you to produce results significantly beyond what you have ever previously been able to achieve.

The five core principles of the Advisory Selling Method are:

Authentic Commitment

Serving a client's best interest at all costs is not easy when we are beset with survival priorities such as paying the bills. It takes a willingness to risk survival for the sake of the fulfillment, recognition, and reward that comes with being of true service to clients.

Genuine Interest

Truly getting to know a client's situation, their desired destination, and what is needed to get them there, in other words their project, requires that we step beyond a comfortable and polite pretense of interest and dive into the risky territory of true interest in another person.

Complete Openness

Being open to whatever outcome will best serve the client means that the client's best interest will be served regardless of the outcome for the trusted advisor. In the end, it turns out that focusing on the client's best interest always comes back to the advisor in the form of repeat business, referrals, and great recommendations. When the client wins, you win.

Fearless Communication

Fearless communication is saying what needs to be said despite the fact it can be risky business. Inviting the inevitable disagreement that emerges when clients hear a truth they don't want to face could jeopardize the relationship. The more you are willing to risk that relationship, the more productive the relationship will become. Since you can't lose what you don't already have, there is nothing to lose, and if you can't risk building a relationship, you will never have one.

Unstoppable Intention

Singular focus on serving a client's best interest requires exercising our power of intention. This is difficult to achieve in the face of daily distractions and emotional reactions that cloud our view of actions that need to be taken. The challenge is to aim your focus solely on a client's best interest and be unstoppable in that intention.

Chapter 8: Generating Opportunities

The First Three Modules of the Advisory Selling Method

Changing how you sell means opening a new doorway to significantly higher income for agents, as trusted advisors, which is a result of shifting your focus off yourself and your agenda onto the client and their project. In order to improve your results, it is essential that you change your actions. In order to change your actions, you must first change who you are being. The starting point on your journey to accomplish this began with the five core principles of Advisory Selling: Authentic Commitment, Genuine Interest, Complete Openness, Fearless Communication, Unstoppable Intention.

The next stop on the road to change is learning, practicing, and applying the practices of the Advisory Selling Method. These are presented module by module and in precise detail both in this chapter and

Chapter 9. By first memorizing the steps, then practicing them in your preparation and execution, you will naturally shift from being a convenience for clients to being a highly valued asset and member of their team.

The Advisory Selling Method offers three modules that generate opportunities. The first taught you how to start from nothing and create viable partnership around a client project. The second taught you how to how to design a powerful presentation. The third guided you in creating the architecture of how the project will be shaped so that there can be a successful launch based on integrity, accountability, and clarity.

Module 1: Building Partnerships

- Practice 1: Evoking Rapport

- Practice 2: Generating Projects

- Practice 3: Forging Partnership

Module 2: Presenting with Power

- Practice 1: Strategic Analysis

- Practice 2: Positioning Value

- Practice 3: Building Presentations

Module 3: Launching Projects

- Practice 1: Defining Challenges

- Practice 2: Designing Projects

- Practice 3: Defining Rules

Chapter 9: Executing Completion

The Final Three Modules of the Advisory Selling Method

Applying the advisory selling deal completion modules is key to ensuring that a project, once launched, is fully realized. The Managing Accountability module is designed to get a deal back on track any time it begins to go in another direction. When a client reaches an impasse in their thinking, the Creating Breakthroughs module empowers the advisor to support the client in getting unstuck. Completing Projects offers a way to go about the transactional business of executing the completion of a project and creating a memorable celebration to acknowledge everyone who contributed. This sets you up for repeat business, referrals, and great recommendations.

Module 4: Managing Accountability

- Practice 1: Establishing Alignment

- Practice 2: Initiating Actions

- Practice 3: Reaffirming Commitments

Module 5: Creating Breakthroughs

- Practice 1: Talking Straight

- Practice 2: Drilling Down

- Practice 3: Rebuilding Trust

Method 6: Completing Projects

- Practice 1: Securing Approvals

- Practice 2: Executing Transactions

- Practice 3: Celebrating Completion

Chapter 10: Changing How You Sell

Taking What You've Learned & Putting It to Work

In this chapter, you learned the difference between forcing a client decision and empowering a client choice. You were then presented with the twelve critical actions that, if taken, will make changing how you sell achievable. Lastly, you learned three models of accelerated learning and high-performance:

Five Steps to Mastery

To master your more natural way of selling it requires the continuous practice of the following five disciplines.

Principles: Creating a principle-based performance method

Practice: Structuring consistent practice following a method

Patience: Developing the patience needed to continue onward

Persistence: Sticking with a learning process no matter what

Passion: Bringing profound joy to the learning process

Knowledge Into Application

The pathway to excellence is paved by the following steps that are required to convert knowledge into effective action and results.

Imitate: Start by doing exactly what has been demonstrated

Integrate: Take what you've learned and start to include it in your approach to make it uniquely yours

Innovate: In response to unpredictable challenges, you must innovate in the moment, going beyond what you've practiced

Incept: Plant a seed in the mind of a client that blossoms in a manner that empowers them and everyone they touch

Inspire: Then, you must draw out the client's ability to act accord with their own best interest and the future possibility they seek

Roadmap to Learning

There are five major obstacles to learning that must be converted into stepping stones to knowledge.

Confusion: I am not sure how a thing is done

Frustration: I know how to do it but am not very good at it

Overwhelm: I can do it well but there is way too much to do

Annoyance: I can do it all but am still not getting it all done

Clarity: I do it well repeatedly but need to get to a new level

A Final Note

Understanding the various stages in your learning process will give you what is needed to push through to a higher level of learning. I have many hopes for you…

…that this book has sparked an awakening to a larger possibility for changing how you sell from unwittingly selling lies to courageously selling the truth and thereby changing everything in your life.

…that you are inspired to dig deeper into the process of uncovering the natural skills within you so you can shift away from the agenda-based approach to selling that dominates our world and limits our effectiveness.

…that you choose to move away from the adversarial path of competition, conspiracy, conflict and corruption that easily devolves into criminality.

…that you allow your natural commitment-based advisory skills to take over so you are more creative, compassionate, collaborative, and more consequential in your contribution to others.

…that you join me on a life-long evolution with respect to how you sell, serve, manage, and perform so that you achieve levels of reward and recognition far exceeding what you may have previously considered to be possible.

There are always risks in making major changes but, if you take responsibility for following the method, your success will blossom fully. I know you can do it and I am committed to helping you make this transition.

If additional support is needed or of interest to you, please take a moment to contact www.advisoryselling.com/contact and we will explore where you currently stand and where you want to take things in the future.

All the best!

Paul

REFERENCE
Principles, Distinctions & Terms

Since the principles, distinctions, and terms we use in the context of Advisory Selling may not match the conventional definitions of Webster or what you learned in school, it became apparent that collecting and organizing some of them would come in handy in your skill development work.

Throughout *Selling the Truth* we have four types of information:

Modular Learning Architecture

The intentional design, building, and function of the various elements of the Advisory Selling Method.

Core Principles

There is a list of Core Principles which are the essential ideas behind Advisory Selling.

Key Distinctions

There is a list of Key Distinctions which are dynamic multilevel principles that generate power in our conversations.

Critical Terms

Finally, there is a list of Critical Terms that define the workings of the Advisory Selling Method.

Modular Learning Architecture

A structure for learning based on alliteration, repetition, and coding. The Advisory Selling Method architecture is composed of a series of modules that contain practices which each have steps. These various elements have specific functions and are meant to shape the language used in a conversation.

Module

A module contains three practices that work together to produce the result of the Module - Generator, Operator, Regulator.

Generator

Launches a conversation in the direction of the objective of the module.

Operator

Serves as the workhorse of the module and does the essential work required to accomplish the purpose of the module.

Regulator

Fulfills the purpose of the module and provides an appropriate transition to other modules.

Practice

Implementation of the Advisory Selling Method in a step-by-step fashion designed to fulfill the intended outcome by use of an intentional language architecture. Each ASM practice within a module has five steps that serve a critical function.

Lead (Step 1)

Sets the direction and steps up to the door to fulfilling the purpose of the practice.

Ground (Step 2)

Brings the conversation down to earth and knocks on the door of the purpose of the practice.

Key (Step 3)

Unlocks the door to the purpose of the practice.

Offer (Step 4)

Opens the door to the next actions that will fulfill the purpose of the practice.

Transition (Step 5)

Steps through the door opened up by the fulfillment of the purpose of the practice, naturally moving into the next practice.

Core Principles

Advisory Selling

Working with clients as a trusted advisor who is genuinely interested in serving the best interest of clients. Advisory Selling agents will stop at nothing to ensure that a client's best interest is served even when their own interest may need to be compromised.

Advisory Selling Principles

Authentic Commitment

Being authentically committed to serving the best interest of clients at all costs.

Genuine Interest

Being genuinely interested in clients including their current and future needs.

Complete Openness

Being completely open to whatever outcome will best serve the client.

Fearless Communication

Being fearless in one's communication with clients, regardless of the risk to the relationship.

Unstoppable Intention

Being unstoppable in one's intention to ensure that the client enjoys a successful outcome.

Advisory Selling Method

A system of six skill development modules, each with three practices that have five steps that are integrated into a dynamic learning architecture that develops the natural advisory skills within people who practice the method.

Agenda-Based Selling

Selling with an agenda, whether hidden or obvious, that will serve the best interest of an agent, even if it's at the expense of a client.

Commitment-Based Advising

Being a trusted advisor who is committed to working with clients to accomplish a project of getting them from where they are currently to where they want to be in the future in a way that serves the client's best interest.

Survival-Driven Human Nature

An unseen automatic adversarial approach to selling which relies upon competition, conspiracy, conflict, and corruption, and may lead to becoming criminal in order to get what one wants.

Service-Driven Human Spirit

Choosing to operate in accord with one's true sense of integrity with creativity, compassion, collaboration, and contribution so that results produced for clients are consequential and establish the foundation for enduring partnerships.

Partnership

The relationship between people who are committed to working collaboratively to accomplish a project critical to their personal, professional, or public future.

Key Distinctions

Definition of Story

A body of interpretations based on past experiences that shapes one's view of the future in a way that limits their actions in the present.

Definition of Selling

Working with clients to create a vision of a future possibility which is compelling enough to change their actions in the present.

Adversarial Selling Techniques

Control Tactics

Control a conversation, overcome objections, and hit some "hot buttons."

Manipulation Tricks

Throw some softening statements, imply an important impending event, and defer to a higher power.

Domination Techniques

Tell people what to think, tell them what to do, and do a tie down to lock them in.

Intimidation Triggers

Create a sense of urgency, forecast a negative outcome, and set an artificial deadline.

Subjugation Traps

Do a takeaway, offer an alternate choice trial close, and make them say thank you.

Incarceration Terms

Secure a written agreement, set a fee schedule, and impose consequences.

Agenda-Based Conversations

Posturing

Positioning oneself as the authority who knows better, even though you may not.

Pretending

Faking it until you make it.

Pressuring

Pushing clients to make a decision that is not in their best interest.

Convincing

Using whatever evidence is available, however questionable, to prove a point.

Forcing Decisions

Aggressively wearing clients down into submission, forcing them to make decisions that serve the agent's best interest.

Commitment-Based Conversations

Positioning

Understanding the true needs of listeners and their vision of the future and positioning a conversation to address these priorities.

Presenting

Making a clear case by offering the full spectrum of available options as to how the client can achieve the results they want and need to produce.

Presencing

Bringing listeners present to the possibility of their success by showing them options they could not previously see.

Recommending

Giving listeners a clear invitation to take appropriate action and making a promise as to the results they will accrue if they accept your invitation.

Empowering Choices

Giving listeners freedom to choose the option that will best help them get from where they are now to where they want to be in the future.

Laws of Human Nature

Competition

Working to win and make others lose.

Conspiracy

Sneaking around to find an advantage.

Conflict

Going to battle to win at others' expense.

Corruption

Cheating in order to win.

Criminal

Knowingly harming opponents to win.

Laws of Human Spirit

Creativity

Approaching challenges with new questions.

Compassion

Being both understanding and intolerant.

Collaboration

Working with people and not against them.

Contribution

Giving your best to others to the fullest.

Consequential

Being a person of consequence to others.

Three Dimensions of Listening

Protective Listening

Automatic reactive listening that protects the listener from the onslaught of selling conversations.

Receptive Listening

Listening that is open and inclusive to ideas that differ from one's current reality.

Inventive Listening

Listening that is seeking to discover new ways of looking at things and how to approach them.

Nature of Reality

Subjective Reality

Interpretations made up in our head that are usually inconsistent with the observable objective facts.

Objective Reality

Observable facts that are not clouded by interpretation.

Creative Reality

The future reality we can create once we are fully present to the objective reality.

Critical Terms

Collaborative Selling

An approach to selling where all parties work toward the greater good in which agents may consider the needs of a client, but still prioritize their own agenda.

Competitive Selling

Working to outsmart clients for one's own gain, and putting clients at a disadvantage in order to make them more dependent on the agent and what they are offering.

Conspiratorial Selling

Using purely deceptive selling to gain inroads with a client so they will fall for a scam, in which they pay mightily for the privilege of causing themselves harm.

Consultative Selling

Selling a solution to a client, whether or not the client has the problem that the solution solves, oftentimes manufacturing a client problem to do so.

Contract Selling

Luring clients into a contract relationship that promises major outcomes in the future but is limited by many disguised conditions that may never deliver the full measure of results originally promised.

Deceptive Selling

Working with clients to create a vision of a future that they are highly unlikely to achieve and possibly damaging the client and killing off any chance of a long-term selling relationship.

Empowering a Choice

The use of an authentic selling style and an eductive mode of influence to bring clients to the point of choosing from an array of options which will best help the client accomplish their project.

Five Levels of Learning

The five levels of learning are confusion, frustration, overwhelm, acceptance, and clarity.

Five Steps to Skill Development

The five steps to skill development are imitate, integrate, innovate, incept, and inspire.

Inceptive Selling

Planting the seed of an idea within the mind of the client that will clearly benefit the client and others they touch in a profoundly positive way that both serves the best interest of the client and achieves the outcomes they intend to produce.

Modes of Influence

There are five modes of influence: Inductive, Deductive, Reductive, Seductive, and Eductive. The Eductive Mode is cultivated by learning the Advisory Selling Method.

Natural Advisory Selling Skills

These skills are building partnerships with clients, packaging power presentations, launching client projects, managing client accountability to keep projects on track, creating client breakthroughs when they get stuck, completing client projects, and celebrating success.

Normal Adversarial Selling Habits

Most sales trainings teach agents control tactics, manipulation tricks, domination techniques, intimidation triggers, and subjugation traps, all in an effort to incarcerate a client with a transactional agreement that they may regret.

Sea of Babble

The unstoppable wave of selling conversations that washes across the planet 24/7, whether in person, on the web, by phone, in print, broadcast media, or social media, with rogue waves that lift people to the top and crash them to the bottom with total lack of mercy.

Selling Strategy

There are five basic selling strategies: aggressive, aversive, apathetic, attentive, and authentic. Only a few choose to be absolutely authentic, the essence of Advisory Selling.

Seven Levels of Being

The seven levels of being are wimp, victim, bozo, player, fool, champion, and master.

CONNECT WITH US!

Congratulations, you are now ready to further develop your Advisory Selling skills. I invite you to contact our team to schedule a free private conversation with me.

We will explore how you can start your journey toward unleashing the full power of your natural advisory selling skills and, by doing so, achieve higher performance, stronger client relationships, and greater financial reward.

Take your next step by contacting us at:

advisoryselling.com/contact

ABOUT THE AUTHOR

Paul's career began in the arts. He illustrated, painted, and created visual effects. He worked on theater design and directed documentaries. Paul was one of two very young people who created the optical effects for the first Star Wars movie. There he had the heady experience of contributing to a project that achieved something that had been thought to be impossible.

Around that time, he realized two things: theater was dying and computer graphic technologies would soon replace film-based optical effects. Paul left the visual arts and the world of stage and screen. He then discovered workshops as a new platform to express all he had learned. He found himself as a director on the stage, speaking and teaching. The stories that unfolded in this venue were about the lives of the people he was working with and how selling shaped their reality. This led to living the very principles presented in this book, honing them along the way.

Paul lives in upstate New York where he enjoys the beauty of nature, delicious food, and an incredible partnership with his wife Brigitte and thrice reincarnated cat Mounette who runs the show.

ACKNOWLEDGMENTS

I would first like to acknowledge my father who was a master salesperson and, when it came to selling, my greatest teacher. His contributions have inspired my contributions, and my contributions are being shared with the intent to inspire yours.

Next I would like to acknowledge the many colleagues and clients I have collaborated with over the past two decades as a professional coach and business consultant. Each experience has honed my clarity regarding what selling could and should look like and has contributed something to the body of work in this book.

Gene Berman is the biggest contributor to the development of the Advisory Selling Method. We spent countless hours together over a twenty-year period developing and testing new ideas about what selling could be, and then I created the practical applications. The results produced by our relationship were astounding, and both he and I, and hundreds of other agents and managers, have achieved high levels of performance and reward.

My first and longest-standing client of over 20 years, Peter Katz, has experienced his gross income grow from a few hundred thousand dollars to over $10 million per year through the course of our relationship. Peter has been a fierce advocate and partner in the development of the Advisory Selling Method.

Ultimately, this book could not exist without the diligent work of my editor, Elizabeth Baker, who was skilled at bringing out what I had to say and passionate about each word. Lisa Traver has been a steadfast full partner in everything I do in business for many years and a strong influence in my writing. Together, from my raw manuscript, they've crafted a book that I am proud to publish.

Beyond this team, there have been many others like Kevin Howe and Ed Madison whose input, insight, and inspiration have made a significant impact. Others who have been instrumental in developing this work from the earliest days include Mike Fasano, Richard Matricaria, Alex Blagojevich, Michael Sullivan, Mike Watson, Still Hunter, David Luther, Brent Smith, Bob Schneiderman, John Barker, Ed Jordan, Brad Balletto, Ari Ravi, Gary Montour, Kirk Felici, Bryn Merry, Adam Tiktin, Greg Matus, Marty Zupancic, Adam Petriella, John Leonard, Howard Hamlin, Matt Sullivan, Brian Hosey, Mark Gjonbalaj, and Bob Horvath.

There is an unnamed multitude of others to thank, and it would take another book to list them all.

So many people, in their own special way, have helped build what I consider to be the most important book to date on selling, one that exposes the truth about what everyone involved in selling deeply wants which is to shift from selling to get recognized and rewarded to truly serving the best interest of others as the means to that end.

www.ingramcontent.com/pod-product-compliance
Lightning Source LLC
Chambersburg PA
CBHW040848210326
41597CB00029B/4768

9 7 9 8 9 8 7 6 6 2 9 0 8